# Breathe Into Breakthrough

# Workbook

Companion to the #1 International Bestselling Book

## Breathe Into Breakthrough

## Elizabeth Borelli

Lasting
Press

First Edition 2022

**ISBN: 978-1-949696-35-6**

Printed in the United States of America

Published by:
Lasting Press
615 NW 2nd Ave #915
Canby, OR 97013

Cover Design, Interior Design, and Launch by Rory Carruthers Marketing
www.RoryCarruthers.com

Special thanks to my editor, Catherine Parisio, and graphic designer Kristin Craig for having my back during the ups and downs of the publishing journey.

For more information about Elizabeth's coaching or programs, or to book her for your next event, speaking engagement, podcast, or media interview, please visit: www.ElizabethBorelli.com

# Table of Contents

# Introduction

*"How you feel depends on the way you use your brain, not the circumstances you're in."*
—Dr. Jill Bolton Taylor, *A Stroke of Insight*

I'm so happy you're here! I hope you're convinced, after reading *Breathe into Breakthrough,* the companion book to this workbook, that a daily mindset alignment practice is the foundation for lasting transformation. If you're ready to go deeper, put aside limiting beliefs, and step into purpose and meaning, this workbook will act as your guide.

In *Breathe into Breakthrough*, we explored in great detail how the mind and body are tied together through the autonomic nervous system. As you continue your growth with this workbook, you'll learn how to use easy and approachable breathwork, movement, and writing exercises as your tools for sustaining change.

Remember that your brain (in its entirety) is most concerned with survival and how your subconscious influences your decisions in favor of this instinct, even when it's completely off base. You'll learn practices for ensuring your goals align with your values and strengths.

Your mind and body are in constant communication. When you're aware of and able to manage the conversation, you're opening the door to new ways to respond to old patterns. This workbook invites you to explore old storylines as you learn to shift your mindset to accommodate new ones.

Please know, if it were easy to change without mindset and resilience training, you would probably have already done it. Change is never linear, but equipped with a heightened awareness, you'll find your way through.

## Why We Can't Seem to Start or Follow Through

As anyone who has attempted to make a big life change knows, it's hard! We start out on a high of excitement and promise, but we can just as quickly come crashing down when we hit the inevitable obstacles that come up whenever we try to replace habits with new ones. Our everyday patterns are so deeply ingrained that much of our behavior is done without a lot of supervision from our conscious awareness.

At first, it's easy to make the case for change and feel resolute in your commitment. But it's hard to keep this in mind when the rubber hits the road. Suddenly, you're back in your old habits and patterns, chalking up your lack of progress to another failed plan or program.

The reality is, even if you wake up in the morning committed to doing things differently, all day long you're hit with stressors, everything from traffic to family to work to finances. Gone unchecked, your stress hormone levels continue to rise as your body keeps this system on high-alert for additional problems. Now you're seeing the world through stress-colored glasses, and the negativity bias this generates keeps you on high alert, long after the initial stressor has passed.

Since stress is both a physical and emotional state, you can't easily snap out of it. So, unless you develop the awareness and tools to intercept these triggering events, your stress level will continue to build throughout the day, driving you to repeat the same patterns.

Breathwork is my tool of choice for building the foundation that helps me increase the awareness of my autopilot thought patterns before they happen. If your normal reaction to traffic is a steady stress buildup all the way to the office, learn to use your breath to stave it off.

Instead of automatically reacting to the stressors that inevitably come your way, you can become aware of your reaction pattern before it's triggered and racing relentlessly down the track. By intercepting early, you can start asking the questions that give you the option to respond differently. Is this traffic really a big deal? Breathe. Does that person's opinion really have the power to make me feel threatened? Breathe. Is this unexpected expense really going to force me to get a second job? Breathe.

In the words of celebrity mega-coach and multi-best-selling author Tony Robbins, "Breath is the ultimate key to your well-being." I call it the gateway to habit change. In my years of coaching people through mid-career and midlife transition, I've learned that unless you learn to regulate your stress response by actively shifting your attention before your involuntary habitual response takes over, you'll end up back at square one.

The beauty of breathwork is it's a twofer. It works both as part of a daily mindfulness practice, which is proven to increase self-awareness, and it is also a great tool for down-regulating stress or boosting energy in the moment, wherever you are. Breathwork is indeed a perfect foundation for a lasting positive mindset shift, but, as we discussed in *Breathe into Breakthrough*, it's not the whole story.

This workbook is designed to provide the tools you need to make lasting change in your life. The exercises will equip you with a proven process for tapping into your strengths, building a strong vision, and resetting your compass towards a path of purpose, power, and potential.

Yes, there will be pitfalls along the way. Change is never linear! But by understanding these normal thought traps and learning mind-body practices for managing emotions, you'll have the tools you need to navigate the road to making your vision a reality and living your best life. Kudos to you for taking the brave first step, and I can't wait to accompany you on your journey!

# Part 1
# Building Your Foundation

## Build a Daily Routine

As discussed in great detail in the *Breathe into Breakthrough* companion book, a daily mindfulness practice like breathwork is strongly correlated with greater focus, emotional intelligence, and resilience. I know from personal and client-reported experience, launching and sustaining lasting change is a mind-body package deal.

If you're reading this and thinking, "enough with the breathwork already," but you haven't started your daily practice, you're in luck. Because I have a story. I did my yoga teacher training with a group of 34 experienced yoga and breathwork practitioners who were committed enough to spend 200 hours of live, camera-always-on instruction on Zoom.

During the training, the instructors emphasized the same advice I can't stress enough, the importance of regular, daily breathing practice for building self-awareness. Granted, I'd been hearing (and even giving) that same advice for many years. Who knows why it took so long to listen, but this time, the advice finally hit home, and I felt ready to commit and see whether a daily practice really would make a difference.

I started small, using the traditional breathing series known as the 4-purifications. The methods are nadi ahodhana (alternate nostril breathing), kapala bhati (breath of fire), agnisara dhauti (bellows breath) and ashvini mudra (a muscle contraction exercise). They are often used as a pathway to meditation.

The whole series only takes about 5 minutes and leaves you feeling focused and energized. I loved this more engaging version of mindfulness meditation and found that, after the breathwork, it was easier to sit in traditional, silent meditation for longer. It took me a while to be able to keep my mind from skipping ahead to the list of things I needed to do and relax into my practice, but I stuck with it, determined not to make perfect the enemy of the good.

As I began to explore breathwork outside of the yoga tradition, I added more practices to my line-up, and my morning routine eventually became my favorite way to start the day.

Several months into the training, during a small group discussion, two of the five people present were discussing how hard it is to find the time for a 20-minute meditation, so they didn't meditate as often as they would have liked. I piped in by sharing the success I was having with my pared-down daily practice. Even if it was just five minutes, it was working for me. Someone chuckled when I said that—it seemed they weren't sure whether I was kidding or not.

Weren't they at the same lectures? Then it dawned on me that I'd heard this same advice from a number of sources, repeated in multiple ways, before finally plugging into it.

Perhaps the person who laughed was in the place of "hearing but not hearing" that I had been in for years. I knew intellectually that a daily mindfulness practice was essential to maintaining lifelong habit changes. Still, I didn't truly understand the benefits deeply enough to put in the effort to make it happen. In hindsight, I can say I wish I'd listened sooner, but the reality is that we each have to grow into our own understanding on our own timeline. Whether or not you follow my advice right away, just by reading this workbook and considering the suggestions, you're one step closer to truly hearing.

Why is daily so important? New habits need frequency and consistency to take hold. Luckily, as I mentioned, a daily practice doesn't take a big time commitment.

Small-and-consistent beats substantial-and-random, so I challenge you to commit to a mindful breathing practice of even as little as five minutes a day, as you build this new habit.

However, even if you're not there yet with your daily practice and even if you're not ready to commit, don't close this book! Start where you're at. Your mind and body are in constant communication, and by tuning in more carefully, you'll build greater self-awareness.

**Laying the Foundation**

Breathwork is a tool for intercepting inner judgments, managing emotions, and aligning your actions with your highest priority goals and values. Yet we don't always remember to use it. We default to autopilot, as we gradually drift back to our routine.

Which is where awareness comes in. It's learning to notice your thoughts and feelings, and how they relate to your physical body. It's important to learn to pay attention to the physical part of yourself as you learn to use your breath, your posture, and your environment to shift your energy, mood, and perception.

Whether you're new to breathwork, or still figuring out how to make it work for you, begin to pay attention to the way you're breathing throughout the day as a way to manage your stress levels. Breathwork is an easy way to shift from stress breath (shallow and fast) to rest-and-digest (deep and slow).

I invite you to pause right now, take a moment to notice if you're breathing deeply or shallowly, how you're sitting or standing, and how you're feeling. Make any adjustments you need to slow and deepen your breath and align your posture, using the mind-body connection to send signals of safety to your brain.

It's hard to understand why something so quick and easy wasn't taught in elementary PE. Simply noticing your breath and checking in with your body throughout the day makes a measurable difference in energy and mood.

## The 365 Pop-Up Breath Check

Now that you know how easy it is to check in with your breath as a way to recognize state or mindset, you can bring this practice into your day as a way to keep stress from building upon itself, as it otherwise would. It's also beneficial to notice your posture, your mood, and your energy level, in case any of those need some adjustment.

3-6-5 is an easy formula for remembering to check in with your breath at least three times a day. When you notice you're breathing through your mouth or high into your chest, make the shift to a nasal breath and slow down as you engage the diaphragm (6 breaths per minute of belly breathing) for five minutes at a time.

Do this three times a day, six breaths per minute, 3-5 minutes at a time=365! This simple exercise brings your body from a state of high stress or low energy back into equilibrium. This practice will also help you to maintain a more positive mindset going forward.

To put this practice into action and establish a routine that becomes a habit, plan ahead. Add a breath check to your calendar or link it to an event, like after a Zoom call, when you're working on something challenging, or when you're stuck in traffic.

To begin, first, assess your breath:
1. Are you breathing through your mouth or your nose?
2. Is your breath fast and shallow or calm and deep?

If you notice that you are breathing fast and shallow, take a moment to slow down and begin to breathe through your nose. Soften your abdomen and let the breath travel down into your lower lungs, as your belly moves in and out with the breath. Pay attention to your breath cycle, slowing it down to equal counts of 4-6 seconds on both the inhale and exhale.

Noticing how you are breathing is the first step to managing your overall anxiety level, and that's not all. By understanding the relationship between the breath and the body, you can use these check-in times to reduce your anxiety, increase your energy, and even tone your muscles and improve your posture.[1]

While I always recommend adding a deep breathing practice to your morning routine, even if you are not ready to take that step, you can sustain your commitment to calm by scheduling several 365 Pop-Up Breath Checks into your day.

Why not start right now by committing to a daily breath check?

**Breathe into Breakthrough Challenge**

Once you decide you are ready to establish a consistent, daily breathing practice, I encourage you to tackle the 10-Day Challenge. The Breathe into Breakthrough 10-Day Challenge invites you to experience the measurable benefits of a daily breathing routine by committing to trying out the technique for at least ten days in a row. Whether you sign up for one of my video workshops or create your own sequence, this is the best way to start small while staying accountable.

The best part? You'll also experience an increase in the "happy hormones:" oxytocin, dopamine, and serotonin. The catch? Your breathing practice is only effective when it becomes a daily ritual, like brushing your teeth or checking your phone. Better yet, you can use it to replace your urge to check your phone or social media account every morning, a surefire way to up-level the way you start your day.

The following breathing exercises are designed to be used individually or in any sequence to open up your airways, balance your autonomic nervous system, and deliver the benefits of a daily mindfulness practice.

---

[1] Dalton, Sarah. "Breathe Deeper to Improve Health and Posture." *Healthline Media*, 23 Oct. 2013, https://www.healthline.com/health/breathe-deeper-improve-health-and-posture#breathing-explained.

You can do these exercises seated or standing, but I recommend finding a quiet space where you won't be disturbed, such as a comfortable chair or a cushion if you prefer the floor, and with hips slightly elevated if you're sitting cross-legged (for comfort). Although you can practice these methods in any position, you'll want to keep a tall spine with your shoulders back and down, unless you're lying down.

For the next ten days, I suggest trying out one new breathing practice a day, using up to four practices per 10-minute session. Choose your favorites, those you find easiest to stay engaged with, as you keep your focus on the breath, leaving any worries, thoughts, or distractions behind. The idea is to find your favorite sequence as you choreograph a practice to best fit your needs.

As I say in my workshops, consistency is key. Find a time you can stick with every day. I recommend mornings, if possible, but before bed is good too. And if you don't have ten minutes, doing five or even two is better than nothing!

Most importantly, don't make "perfect" the enemy of "good!" If your mind wanders during practice, that's normal. As long as you're showing up for yourself, you can't do this wrong.

Remember, this is a new habit, and your survival brain will attempt to derail you by convincing you it won't work, you're not doing it right, or you don't have time. Don't let that happen!

Tips for success:
- Commit to sticking with the practice for at least ten days (or as many more as you like!) with an open mind.
- Make it a first-thing-in-the-morning priority, even if you just have five minutes some days.
- Make sure your space is comfortable and quiet!
- Make the new habit your own by trying out different practices until you find those that work for you.

**Breathing Exercises for Your Daily Routine**

There are hundreds of breathing exercises out there, from yoga-based to military-devised. Yes, box breathing was devised by a soldier to help keep the troops calm and is one of the methods used by the armed forces today. Those included here are a compilation of exercises I use and recommend for their ease and accessibility.

This is a summary of the breathing practices designed to be used as a guide for building your daily routine. You can find the full exercise details in Chapter 12 of *Breathe into Breakthrough*. Try different combinations to find the sequence that works best for you.

### 1. The 3-Part Breath

This is the foundational practice I always teach first. This breath creates a state of mental alertness, even as it activates the parasympathetic nervous system to calm the mind.

### 2. Box Breathing

A simple yet powerful technique for down-regulating stress and improving focus.

### 3. The 4-7-8 Breath

Popularized by Dr. Andrew Weil, this breathing practice triggers the relaxation response in the autonomic nervous system. It's quick and easy enough to use whenever you experience tension or stress.

Once you add this technique to your everyday practice, you'll find it helpful for preventing a stress response in the first place. The effects are subtle at first try but become more pronounced with repetition and practice. The 4-7-8 breath is also an effective tool for falling asleep.

### 4. Breathing in Steps (*Exhale-extended version*)

Exhale-extended breathing calms your autonomic nervous system (ANS). This breathing pattern is a great way to introduce breath-holding patterns into your practice.

**5. Breathing in Steps** (*Inhale-extended version*)

Inhale-extended breathing stimulates your autonomic nervous system (ANS). This is a great alternative to Breath of Fire if you find that practice agitating.

**6. Alternate Nostril Breathing**

This is one of my daily, go-to breathing practices for starting my morning and calming in the face of stress. A few minutes of breathing in a calm, rhythmic pattern through one nostril at a time brings your autonomic nervous system (ANS) into balance and downregulates your emotional state.

**7. Breath of Fire**

This more advanced breathing method involves partial breath retention combined with rapid nasal breathing, with a focus on chest breath. This active breathing method is a highly effective way to help you focus your energy prior to meditation and is often practiced in combination with Bellows Breath and Alternate Nostril Breathing.

**8. Bellows Breath**

This active breath-holding practice is both calming and energizing. Isolating the belly, you'll pull your abdominal muscles in and out to create a wave-like deep pumping action that massages the intestines and gently stimulates the autonomic nervous system when combined with deep breathing. Best done first thing in the morning on an empty stomach as part of your daily practice.

**9. Tummo or Wim Hof Style Breathing (advanced practice)**

This deep breathing and holding practice is proven to help regulate stress levels, boost metabolism, and improve vascular health.

**10. Relaxing Body Scan**

This exercise was developed by Jon Kabat-Zinn at the University of Massachusetts, Amherst Medical School to manage stress and chronic pain. Also, a great way to relax your mind and body before bedtime, this practice can help you begin to recognize and process difficult memories and emotions you may be subconsciously holding onto.

Through this exercise, you are creating a larger awareness and acceptance of your body. Later, if you experience difficult memories or emotions, the body scan creates a safe method for processing the feelings that arise, labeling them and letting them go, allowing you to return to a place of self-compassion.

**Bonus: Self-Acceptance Meditation**

This is a beautiful way to remind yourself that you are enough. In truth, most of us can't hear this message too frequently. It's human nature to compare and judge ourselves (and others). But the extent of our ability to love and accept ourselves boosts the amount of love and acceptance we have to share with others.

To move into meditation, when you've finished your breathing exercises close your eyes and keep your focus on the path of your breath. You don't need to change it, simply keep your awareness on it as it travels through a soft-belly breathing pattern.

Now begin silently repeating the words "I am" on the inhale, and "enough" on the exhale. Continue this repetition for at least five breaths.

Now see if you can envision your face, as though you're looking at yourself in the mirror. This time switch the words slightly to "You are" on the inhale, and "enough" on the exhale. Continue this repetition for at least five breaths.

Finally, think of someone or everyone you know in need of compassion. See if you can envision them as you change the phrase to "We are" on the inhale, and "enough" on the exhale. Continue this repetition for at least five breaths.

This practice of silently repeating words or phrases in time with the breath during meditation is called a mantra. You can use any words that feel healing or helpful. It's an approachable way to meditate and align your daily focus.

**Establishing Your Practice**

*Remember*, the most important part of any breathing practice is just to DO IT. Any combination of exercises is beneficial, and I suggest you experiment a bit until you find a routine that works for you. If you'd like a little help getting started, here are some examples of routines that provide a good balance of exercises.

**Example of a beginner's daily (5-15 minute) routine:**
- The 3-Part Breath
- Alternate Nostril Breathing or 4-7-8 Breath
- Box Breathing or Breathing in Steps
- Ending with the Self-acceptance Mediation is optional

**Example of an intermediate daily (10-15 minute) routine:**
- The 3-Part Breath
- Alternate Nostril Breathing or 4-7-8 Breath
- Breath of Fire or Breathing in Steps, inhale-focused
- Bellows Breath or Box Breathing
- Meditation (5+ minutes)

**Example of an advanced daily (15-20 minute) routine:**
- Wim Hof Style Breathing
- Alternate Nostril Breathing
- Breath of Fire
- Bellows Breath
- Meditation (8+ minutes)

**How Real Does It Get?**

If thoughts are based on perceptions, how fixed is reality? *Perception **is** reality,* one of my friends said about her ex's most recent eyebrow-raiser. "I always do everything," the ex had shouted at her after being asked to drive their daughter to dance rehearsal.

I'm sure his statement was valid; in his mind, he thought he did do everything. And that fact is probably on the list of reasons they're now divorced. Our perceived reality is truly subjective.

We each regard our own interpretations as fact, but in reality, our version of what is truly going on in the world is unique to each of us, influenced by our beliefs, values, moods, and histories. Even identical twins see the same things differently based on their individual past experiences.

You are probably familiar with the studies involving two people who have witnessed the same event, only to describe it very differently afterward, each with equal certainty that their account was the right one. How does that happen? Was one person not paying attention? Or did they both get it wrong? Just how accurate is our perception? The answer might surprise you!

I hate to break it to you, but your version of reality isn't an objective reflection of the input coming from your five senses. Your interpretation is a mixture of internal and external circumstances, your current state of mind, and your long-held patterns. This is a really important recipe to remember when we examine our perceptions, beliefs, and judgments.

- Internal circumstances: biological needs, hormones, current level of stress, memories of similar past events
- External circumstances: environment, physical comfort, safety, other people
- Current state of mind: distracted, alert, triggered, excited, bored, annoyed, interested, curious

- Long-held processing patterns: how you usually respond to similar circumstances, your personality

As you can see, there are a lot of individually subjective ingredients in the mix. The result is your unique narrative, your story. This holds true for events that you observe in the world, and it also plays a role in how you view yourself and your own life.

But fortunately, your circumstances, state of mind, and long-held patterns are all within your control. Through breathwork training, mind-body practices, and a commitment to make meaningful changes in your life, you can empower yourself to expand your vision of what is possible.

Ultimately, you're the author of your own story, the one you tell, the one you believe, and sometimes the one you get stuck in. If you're here, I'm guessing you're ready to change a part of your story. You know your own beliefs are holding you back, yet no matter how hard you try, you can't think your way out of it. Why not? Are you not disciplined, smart, or confident enough? What's wrong with you?

The good news is absolutely nothing is wrong with your perception. In fact, it's your brilliant biology at work. Your brain is hardwired to prioritize safety and connection, which is how humans survived as a species for all these millennia. With all of the unknowns, putting yourself out there feels like the biggest risk you could ever take.

Your "survival brain," the oldest region of the multipart structure of your mind, is the first line of defense when it comes to threat management. Its goal is to keep you safe in your comfort zone by throwing up limiting beliefs that make up the framework for keeping you inside your current storyline.

Beliefs like, "*I could never do that,*" or "*Why would anyone listen to me?*" or "*I'm not (fill in the blank) enough,*" or "*I'm too old,*" (a saying I've heard dozens of times said by clients a lot younger than me!) all stop us from moving forward. We hold off on making a change, yet we end up feeling as stressed about not changing as we would if we took the risk.

Sometimes we get convinced that the stress is helping us to stay motivated, but all it's really doing is driving us to stay busy all day doing things that don't get us closer to our goals.

I know all about this firsthand. For most of my adult life, it was all I could do to push myself out of my comfort zone like a drill sergeant, just to keep convincing myself I could do it. The list of businesses, projects, and challenges I undertook kept growing. Although I consistently lived and even succeeded outside of my comfort zone, my internal story of anxiety was what drove my behavior. So instead of focused growth and progress, I was just spinning in circles, jumping into something new each time I became bored or frustrated with my latest passion project.

As I began practicing daily breathwork and using the other mind-body exercises to manage my emotions as they came up, I began to gain clarity around the way I was undermining my long-term goals with short-term busywork. Even though I was taking action, I was still stuck in a pattern that wasn't allowing me to make progress towards my bigger picture goals.

Let me describe a typical workday for you. I always start with my early morning wellness and family check-in routine, then head to my office to start my workday. I skim my daily calendar for meetings and to-do items.

Before I got really clear in aligning my big-picture goals with daily priorities, I would start my day on LinkedIn, "networking." *It's important!* I told myself. I would like, respond, share, and post. I thought this would bring clients to my website. It didn't. Then I looked at my website. Why weren't clients clamoring to it? Maybe I should change the colors. How about writing an article to post to Medium? Maybe that would get some attention.

Suddenly the day was over and busy as I was, I hadn't engaged with prospective clients or made progress on the training videos I'd had on my to-do list for weeks. Why? Because those things were intimidating. So, I put them off in a cloud of busywork and my coaching business stayed stagnant. It was almost laughable when I listened to Rich Litvin's bestselling (audio)book, *The Prosperous Coach,* as he described my day to a tee. In fact, I did start laughing! I was doing the very thing I always help clients to see in themselves; engaging in busywork as a way to avoid the hard stuff.

I immediately shifted strategies to reallocate the time I spent social media "networking," writing and rewriting my tagline, or beautifying my website to low priority status, and began looking at what I was avoiding because I "wasn't ready", or I felt "too old," or it "didn't have the right setting."

Reorienting my priorities made a huge difference, not only in my business, but in my sense of well-being. I finally took the plunge and began offering live workshops teaching breathwork techniques, which people gravitated to and engaged with. It was scary as hell, and all my saboteurs (remember them from *Breathe into Breakthrough*?) showed up, but I used my own breathing and mindfulness practices to stay the course. I knew the classes wouldn't be perfect, but I also knew I had to start before I was ready, put a stake in the ground, and build up from there.

My first videos were awkward, to say the least, but I kept going. As I developed my programs, I began reaching out to educators and influencers who use breathwork and mind-body practices in professional settings. I was amazed at the positive reception I received; so much support and guidance!

Since then, I've expanded my ability to share this work. I've been invited to speak at multiple summits, and even had the opportunity to present with a group of esteemed breathwork experts in Cabo at the Breathing Festival. This transformation, from spinning my wheels and not making much progress to a whirlwind of activity and growth in my business, happened over the course of a year, fueled by my passion for this work and my ability to face my fears and manage my limiting beliefs.

The goal of this workbook is to help you identify your limiting beliefs and understand how they create the outer limits of possibility in your story. From there, you will discover how your everyday habits, from sleep to breath to movement, can shift to help you break through them.

## Which Lens Are You Looking Through?

How you see one thing is how you see everything. And left to its own devices, your brain prefers to err on the side of caution. After all, our most basic drive is survival. And in survival brain, everything looks like a potential threat.

In this state, we stay on high alert, deflecting one problem, one issue, one situation after another. We feel overwhelmed and busy, but never able to find time to address the things we deeply care about.

Uncertainty drives this state, and when we're in it, it's hard to see any other option. We feel stuck and anxious, which keeps the pathway activated and the Thinking Brain (illustrated in the diagram below) shut out.

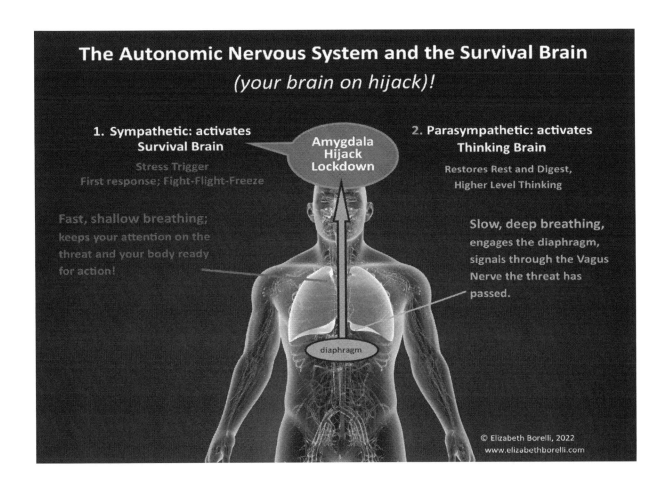

This diagram illustrates the differences between your brain *on hijack* and the productive, thinking brain. The challenge is that stress triggers your survival brain, and change — the process of leaving your comfort zone, putting yourself out there, taking a risk — and the state of vulnerability this creates, is stressful.

**Take the Body-Mind Pathway to Calm**

It's easy to assume our feelings develop from the thinking brain, and that they're logical, rational, and right. But that's a whole lot to expect of our senses. After all, they're not purely logic-based. Your body has a major influence in how you feel, which effects the way you think.

When you're hungry, it's easy to become "hangry," when you're tired, it's hard to feel enthused. And when you're stressed? Your body responds as your system shifts to prepare to fight, fly or freeze. So even though you're not in immediate danger, it's hard to focus, relax, or stay energized. Even if the stressor is your partner, your job, or the morning news.

When your body is sending stress signals, you can't think your way out of the fear response. Luckily there is another pathway, a more direct channel we can use to move our minds from a stress state into a more balanced perspective. It's the nerve known as vagus, and it connects the organs with the senses as it passes information back and forth to make sure you're safe and connected.

The vagus nerve is a central communications channel between the brain and body, extending from what's known as the gut-brain axis, the brainstem down into your stomach and intestines.

The vagus nerve plays an important role in the gut-brain axis, affecting not only your mood, but it also has been implicated in the development of depression and anxiety. Another study, published in the same journal, noted that vagus nerve stimulation may be an additional therapy for treatment-resistant depression and posttraumatic stress disorder. (Of course, these exercises are not a substitute for treatment your provider has recommended for you.)[2]

When you're caught up in your emotions; anxious, angry, or shut down from stress, you can access the vagus nerve, using a combination of breathwork and simple movement practices.
It may not surprise you to learn that conscious breathing, especially practices that engage the diaphragm, is the top recommendation for accessing the vagus nerve and intercepting a stress response. Here are two simple methods for tapping into this amazing resource:

---

[2] Breit, Sigrid, et al. "Vagus Nerve as Modulator of the Brain–Gut Axis in Psychiatric and Inflammatory Disorders." *Frontiers in Psychiatry,* vol. 0, Jan. 2018, https://doi.org/10.3389/fpsyt.2018.00044.

- Conscious Breathing: The most immediate way to change the balance of sympathetic and parasympathetic nervous system actions is with the breath. Research has found that slow, rhythmic, diaphragmatic breathing increases healthy vagal tone.[3]
- Adding sound. When we hum or sing, the vagus nerve is activated— which is one of the reasons why those activities can be so cathartic. Engaging in conscious breathing and adding a humming sound on your exhale is a great way to further engage your vagus.

Your mindset is critically dependent on the state of the sensory input your body feeds into it. Understanding this relationship takes time. Developing greater conscious awareness of our internal experiences which are both a result of our external environment and internal biological dynamics.

While we can't always influence the external environment, each one of us has the tools we need to build our internal awareness and tap into our natural state of calm.

**What Comes Up for You When You Think about Starting Something New?**

When we think of taking a risk, leaving the familiar for the unknown, most of us struggle with confidence, clarity, and motivation. As a result, our own judgment of ourselves or of the situation makes us feel overwhelmed and scattered, which prevents us from taking action.

The longer we continue to wallow in self-doubt, the more convinced we are that these limiting beliefs are true. The irony in all this is, in trying to avoid the pain, we're fueling the survival brain's stories, making us feel even more anxious, stressed, and stuck.

---

[3] Lehrer, Paul M., and Richard Gevirtz. "Heart Rate Variability Biofeedback: How and Why Does It Work?" *Frontiers in Psychology*, vol. 0, Jan. 2014, https://doi.org/10.3389/fpsyg.2014.00756.

So, until we can understand how the survival brain keeps us stuck within this framework, this story that's not working for us, we'll never be ready to commit to our vision, or even to get clear about what we want. Because we can't think our way out of this box.

The good news is we don't have to rely on the brain to set us free from survival mode. The body can just as easily drive the brain to drop the defenses long enough to consider less urgent, less impulse-driven action. Maybe you're not ready to leave your comfort zone entirely, but when you can disconnect from the stress/survival brain, you'll begin to recognize new options that feel doable, inspiring, or clarifying, as you begin taking the first step, and then the next one, gaining more confidence every time you take action.

Sounds kind of easy, right? It would be if change was linear. You could steadily progress one step at a time, moving gracefully from stuck to unstoppable. The problem is your brilliant brain is a master at keeping you as pain-free as possible. This means, unless you're paying very close attention, your survival response will continue to sneak in and sabotage your efforts with harsh judgments like "*You're not ready*" or "*You might fail*" or "*It's too late*" (more on these voices later) before you can intervene.

Until we learn to recognize and tune into our signals, our stress level can begin to rise as soon as we get up in the morning, when we immediately return to yesterday's problems, picking right up where we left off. Unless we take time to check-in and use a breathing or mindfulness exercise to reduce our stress, it will often keep rising. This results in you feeling anxious or disappointed in yourself for not doing or accomplishing more. So, when the progress you did make doesn't measure up to your expectations, you toss out the baby with the bathwater and go back to your negative but comfortable way of thinking. *See, I knew I wasn't cut out for this.* And the dopamine hit you get from being right in your true, albeit negative, prediction seals the deal.

So, this anxiety-driven thought loop keeps you feeling stuck. And trying without succeeding feels like abject failure, instead of the normal ups and downs of progress. Change is never linear.

But here's the reality, personal development isn't the same as yo-yo dieting. If you fall off the wagon, your progress isn't lost. And when you get back on that wagon the next time, you'll recapture the benefit of that initial ride. So, you only start from scratch once, because your efforts are cumulative and will keep building until you no longer have to worry about wagons, and you're over that bridge.

How can we use the mind-body connection to intercept this negative thought treadmill that seems to be holding us hostage? You won't be surprised to hear that breathwork is a top recommendation.

**Soft Belly Exercise**

(*Allow 5+ minutes to complete this exercise*)

One useful exercise, promoted by my friend Dr. James Gordon, former Presidential wellness council and founder of the Center for Mind Body Medicine. This go-to technique is known as Soft Belly, and I use it often.

Think of it as a "concentrative meditation" a mind-body practice to quiet the stress response, making it easier for us to accept and put our emotions in perspective. This movement stimulates certain regions of the brain that enable us to detangle from and gain perspective on our emotions. We can acknowledge it without buying into it. We can separate our emotional responses from what we know today. When we're able to access the parasympathetic nervous system with Soft Belly, we are able, little by little, to quiet the feeling of being triggered, or stress, or like your life is out of your control. The result is that we're able to react less and respond more. Ready to try it out?

1. Sit in a comfortable position on the floor or in a chair.
2. Straighten your spine, move your shoulders back and down, and begin breathing through your nose.
3. As your breath flows in, feel it move down into your belly.
4. On your inhale, think, "soft," allowing your belly to receive your breath.
5. On your exhale, think, "out," as you begin slowing the pace of your breath.
6. Continue with this steady pattern until you feel present and grounded.

Use this exercise throughout the day to keep stress in check or move from survival to thinking brain whenever you feel your stress level rising.

**Raising Awareness: Get to Know Your Go-To Emotions**

When you're stuck or trapped in an unhappy or unfulfilling situation, it could be because you've come up against the bars of your limiting beliefs. For example, change leads us into uncertain territory. The unknown can be scary for many, if not most, people. Rather than face our fear and risk feeling like a failure, we tell ourselves we don't have time, or it's not the right time, or whatever your go-to reason happens to be. So now, instead of feeling fear of change or failure, you feel resentful, angry, or overwhelmed.

Your brilliant brain, devoted to keeping you from having to face such painful feelings (fear), serves up more acceptable decoy feelings (anger, overwhelm) to keep you from emotional harm.

Best-selling author and celebrity psychologist, Lori Gottlieb, calls these feelings "surface" emotions. These are the feelings you express while really masking deeper inner feelings around self-worth. So, you avoid the fear and stick with the resentment, frustration, anger, and overwhelm. But every time you heed those inner voices telling you all the reasons why you're trapped in a situation you can't change, you shut down an opportunity for growth.

Like in my case, in which I didn't even realize I was avoiding the things I most needed to do (and which I subconsciously feared doing) by staying distracted with busywork. When you are deep in avoidance behavior it can be hard to see the forest through the trees. But even when you're aware of your negative thinking patterns, it's difficult to think your way out of your limiting beliefs. But we can gain much more traction and move ahead if we can identify our true feelings and locate the source of these emotions in the body.

Let's say, for example, you're feeling stuck in a role where you're underpaid, undervalued, or no longer challenged. You're ready to either advance in your current job or find a new one. So, you begin looking at job descriptions, and you start to feel short of breath. You notice that you're missing at least 2-3 requirements from every job you look at. You get overwhelmed, triggered into your same old storyline; you have too much to do right now to deal with this, and you decide you're not ready to make a drastic change. You'll just stay where you're at for now.

On the surface, you've told yourself a story that places the blame for your inertia on outside circumstances (too busy!), but behind the scenes, your body is signaling a fear response driven by the survival brain, which is doing its job of keeping you safe from failure. But because you're in survival brain, everything feels like a threat, so now you're overwhelmed and just want to stop feeling this way. So, you accept the lack-of-time belief as fact, instead of pausing to get curious about what's really going on.

Another result of stress-induced overwhelm is what I call the Kitchen Sink. Meaning, once one thing goes wrong, everything else gets dumped into the nothing's-going-right sink along with it. When we're in this place of stress, we begin noticing and running through a list of all the things that are going wrong in our lives. And they all seem to be demanding our attention at once. So, we can't focus. We can't even think straight, and we definitely don't have the time or the bandwidth to prioritize our goals while everything continues to pile up in the kitchen sink.

As we've been learning, what we perceive to be true creates our reality, which, as you recall, is a byproduct of internal and external signals, our current state of mind, and our long-held processing patterns. Our reality is shaped by our limiting beliefs, but once we recognize them for what they are (beliefs, not facts), they begin to lose their power. We still hear that voice, but now we understand what it's trying to do and why, and we don't have to listen to it. And the less we listen, the smaller it becomes.

## Navigating Your Emotional Landscape

The tricky thing about emotions is that we often misread them. Not only in others, but in ourselves. Emotions are not straightforward. In the language of surface emotions, anger is often a cover for pain. Fear hides behind frustration. Apathy may mask sadness. The emotions we find most difficult to deal with often get redirected so they're less painful.

In *Breathe into Breakthrough,* we talked about my client who lost his job and misdirected the pain of rejection into anger at his former company. That's perfectly normal. But it's also a dead-end road. Uncovering our hidden emotions lets us better understand them. Once we know the true emotions at the core of our reaction, we can apply the compassion we deeply need in order to be able to accept what we are feeling and then let those emotions go.

We often underestimate the way our bodies collaborate with our brains to strengthen our emotional responses. We intuitively know where stress lives in our systems—the butterflies in our stomachs, the muscle tension in our shoulders, the faster heartbeat—all signal the fear response, often before our brain even registers the feeling.

Yet, we're less aware of subtler signals. You may have read the research tying specific physical movements to certain emotions, as in the smile studies which determined that emotional responses were influenced by factors as subtle as the shape of one's month. Research shows if you hold a pencil between your teeth (which causes you to smile) while looking at a cartoon, you're likely to find it funnier. Less well-known is the huge impact physical states such as your posture can have on your mood. Poor posture can lead to lower self-esteem and energy levels, while good posture can contribute to an increase in confidence and alertness, among other benefits.

This dialogue between body and brain is ongoing, yet usually takes place outside of our awareness. Tuning into physical sensations gives us a tangible experience to work with. As we learned in *Breathe into Breakthrough*, research shows that emotions have a physical blueprint. Even those feelings you think are all in your head still create sensations in the rest of your body. When we direct our attention to these feelings, we can use breathwork to dial down the response, and a Letting Go practice, like you'll learn on page 38, to open the door to more helpful perspectives.

**Uncovering Your Primary Emotions**

The following exercise is designed to help you connect with your deeper emotions. Often when we're feeling overwhelmed or stressed, we are unable to pinpoint our core feelings, which tend to be less acceptable, both culturally and even to ourselves. Yet understanding and connecting with these deeper emotions helps us accept them and let them go in a healthier way.

Take a look at the chart below and circle the primary emotions or feelings that first come up for you when you think about regrets in your life. These emotions may include:

| | | |
|---|---|---|
| • Disappointment | • Sadness | • Frustration |
| • Compassion | • Hurt | • Irritation |
| • Fear | • Guilt | • Impatience |
| • Shame | • Overwhelm | • Pain |
| • Anxiety | • Stress | • Self-doubt |
| • Resentment | • Restlessness | • Dissatisfaction |

These primary emotions often mask feelings that we're subconsciously suppressing. Read through the next list slowly and with curiosity. See if you are feeling any of these secondary emotions, which may include:

| | | |
|---|---|---|
| • Disapproval | • Paranoia | • Insecurity |
| • Disdain | • Distrust | • Low Self Esteem |
| • Hatred | • Jealousy | • Self-hatred |
| • Hostility | • Worry | • Depression |
| • Victim Complex | • Anxiety | • Anger/Rage |

It can be challenging to examine painful feelings, yet looking at these deeper emotions gives us the opportunity to meet them with compassion. In a process known as interoception, or turning our attention inward, we can learn to notice, label, and let go of these hidden feelings without buying into them.

Building greater awareness of the relationship between our emotional state and our physical feelings gives you the power to hack out of a stress state through your physical body, instead of trying to think your way out of it. This is the gateway to managing your emotions so you can control them instead of letting them control you.

**Hello Emotions Exercise**

As you go through your day, make it a point to check in with your emotional state and use your phone or a notepad to write down in a word or two how you're feeling. Hint, if you connect this to another 3-time a day habit, like at mealtimes or right before your breath check, you're more likely to remember to do it. Do this for a week and then take a look at the feelings you wrote down and respond to the following.

List the three most common emotions you experience on a daily basis, both negative and positive:

_____

_____

_____

When you experience the emotions you listed above, where do they show up in your body? Do the feelings manifest as excitement, sleepiness, alertness, sensitivity, tension, pain, shakiness, numbness, or something else? On the lines below, explain when you feel these common emotions and how the feeling manifests. I've provided a couple of my own examples.

**Example 1:** When I prepare to teach a workshop, I feel excitement, which shows up in my heart region.

_____

_____

_____

**Example 2:** When my partner talks down to me, I feel a knot in the pit of my stomach that I know is anxiety.

_____

_____

_____

**Example 3:** When I feel overwhelmed with too much to do, sometimes I feel like my head is spinning and it's hard to focus.

_____

_____

_____

If you could change one negative reaction and the feeling it brings up, which would it be? And why?

**Example:** I would like to learn to control the feeling of overwhelm because when I feel that way, I get paralyzed and end up getting nothing done, which just makes me feel bad about myself.

_____

_____

_____

Remember, awareness is the first step to changing habits. Knowing when you're likely to be triggered gives you the opportunity to plan your response ahead of time.

## Part 2

## Getting to Know Yourself

**Core Values Exercise**

Core values are the fundamental beliefs or guiding principles which dictate behavior and help people navigate their choices between right and wrong. No news there! But too often we let distractions or demands derail us from our priority goals before we've had time to ask, "Was answering that call important enough to miss my morning window, or could I have listened to how frustrated my friend is with her partner later that day?"

Core values help us to determine if we are on the right path to fulfilling our goals by creating an unwavering guide. These fundamental guiding principles generally remain stable throughout most of our lives, but when our focus changes, our priorities shift as well. Habits and routines that used to align with our values and goals may no longer serve us, so it's important to check in with yourself periodically.

Maybe previously a top priority was making breakfast for your kids, but now that they're 12 and 14, do you really need to miss your self-care time for something they can easily do themselves? Time for a values check!

Maybe you've realized that treating yourself to a nightly hour of Netflix keeps you from getting up early enough to make time for yourself in the morning. Since you've been feeling tired and stressed as a result, it's time for a values shift. After weighing the options, you might decide to prioritize self-care by starting a morning breathing practice. Instead of going cold turkey on Netflix, you will start your show a half hour earlier.

Whether we're merely thinking about a change or already in the process of transition, old habits often continue to dictate our routines. This is why it's important to check-in every so often, so these decisions don't make themselves.

In the following list, circle ten words that you feel most closely describe your personal and professional values:

| Personal Values | Professional Values |
|---|---|
| Creativity | Flexibility |
| Adventure/Fun/Humor/Spontaneity | Financial Security |
| Curiosity | Stability |
| Honesty/Candor/Integrity | Engagement/Challenge |
| Humility | Meaning/Purpose/Inspiration |
| Beauty | Recognition |
| Nature | Appreciation |
| Authenticity | Independence |
| Intelligence/Knowledge | Diversity |
| Education/Learning | Inclusion |
| Compassion/Kindness/Love/Consideration | Leadership |
| Forgiveness | Responsibility |
| Charisma/Friendliness/Warmth | Balance |
| Listening/Communication | Autonomy |
| Confidence | Listening |
| Gratitude | Communication |
| Generosity | Creativity |
| Logic/Rationality | Innovation |
| Courage | Social justice |
| Social justice/Fairness | Environmental impact |
| Optimism | Fairness |
| Respect/Thoughtfulness | Respect |
| Open-mindedness | Candor |
| Self-control/Willpower | |
| Organization | |
| Spirituality | |
| Patience | |
| Perseverance/Hard work/Persistence | |

Now review what you circled. Choose the top 2 or 3 you feel represent values you most closely relate to or want to cultivate in your personal life, and the top 2 or 3 you want to prioritize in your professional life (if applicable). List them below:

**My top priority personal values are:**

_____

_____

_____

**My top priority professional values are:**

_____

_____

_____

**Think about the values in each of these categories.**

When and where do these values show up in your life?

_____

_____

_____

Where are they missing?

_____

_____

_____

As we move through the workbook, we'll refer back to these values, making sure they're part of your vision and action plan.

**Managing the Judge**

As we've seen, our brain is always on the lookout for danger, which is why we've survived, both individually and as a race. So, we've much to be grateful for! Yet our brains, in service of our safety, err on the side of caution. Our survival brain is much more comfortable when we stay safely in the confines of our comfort zone. Yet our thinking brain knows we need to take some risks in order for growth to happen.

As long as we're on our game, in control and on track with our plans, all is right with our mindset. Yet during the inevitable challenges associated with change, our survival brain turns up in ever so sneaky ways with our innate tendency toward self-sabotage.

As we've seen, our minds and bodies are constantly judging, assessing every new situation for clues about your—you guessed it—safety. This is why we're wired to make immediate judgments even before our brains have had time to consciously process the new information.[4] In the brain's quest to keep you safe at all costs, it makes sense to react quickly without necessarily thinking things through. And since humans have a natural bias for negativity, guess which half glass you're most likely to grab?[5]

Of course, sometimes having an immediate reaction is enormously beneficial. Your brain is wired to prepare you to jump out of the way of a speeding biker before you have time to get distracted by the details. Which is perfect when there really is a speeding biker or some other real danger, but it can be debilitating when your unconscious mind prevents you from taking the necessary risks in pursuit of your goals.

---

[4] University of Melbourne. "Judgment and decision-making: Brain activity indicates there is more than meets the eye." ScienceDaily. ScienceDaily, 2 October 2014. <www.sciencedaily.com/releases/2014/10/141002101218.htm>.

[5] Cherry, Kendra. "Why Our Brains Are Hardwired to Focus on the Negative." *Verywell Mind*, 11 Apr. 2019, https://www.verywellmind.com/negative-bias-4589618.

These self-sabotaging thoughts are caused by what Positive Intelligence theory labels "Saboteurs." Saboteurs are the voices in your head that generate your go-to negative responses to life's everyday challenges. They represent your deeply-ingrained, automated patterns for how to think, feel, and respond. The resulting stress, anxiety, self-doubt, frustration, restlessness, and unhappiness can sabotage everything from your performance, to your wellbeing, to your relationships.

Formed in early childhood, these Saboteurs helped you survive physically and emotionally growing up. However, they greatly limit your potential as an adult.[6]

As discussed in *Breathe into Breakthrough*, we all have different go-to patterns of self-sabotage that show up when we're triggered, often before we can stop them. Below is the list of the ten most common negative response patterns, according to Positive Intelligence theory:

1. **The Judge (the master saboteur):** Compels us to find fault with ourselves, others, and our conditions and circumstances
2. **The Stickler:** Compels us to take our need for perfection, order, and organization to an extreme
3. **The Pleaser:** Compels us to gain acceptance by constantly helping, pleasing, and rescuing others
4. **The Hyper-Achiever**: Compels us to pursue constant performance and achievement for self-validation
5. **The Victim:** Compels us to feel that bad things always happen to us and use our 'poor me' message as a way of gaining attention
6. **The Hyper-Rational**: Compels us to have an intense and exclusive focus on the rational and analytical aspects of everything, including relationships
7. **The Hyper-Vigilant:** Compels us to feel intense anxiety about all the dangers and uncertainty surrounding us

---

[6] "Saboteurs." *Positive Intelligence*, 26 Nov. 2021, https://www.positiveintelligence.com/saboteurs/.

8. **The Restless:** Compels us to constantly be in search of greater excitement through perpetual busyness
9. **The Controller:** Compels us to take charge and control situations and other people
10. **The Avoider:** Compels us to avoid difficult and unpleasant tasks and conflicts

The first step in weakening your Saboteurs is to identify and expose them, as you can't fight an invisible enemy, especially one pretending to be your friend. Yet the most common among all of them is the Judge. We know that uncertainty, like that which we experience when stepping out of our comfort zone, activates the survival brain. What we are going to explore now is how the extra dose of anxiety this delivers creates a recipe for self-judgment disaster.

For example: You started a new job, and you're having coffee with your manager. You're a bit anxious, and you make a response during the conversation you thought sounded stupid. After you leave, the thought nags you. You're not sure you said the right thing, so you keep playing the event over and over in your mind, cringing as you chastise yourself for ever making that comment.

This is when the thought loop replay, also known as rumination, kicks in.

Now before you know it, you're stuck in a thought pattern that's hard to break, and you have no idea whether the comment was even noticed, or if it was, how it actually reflected on you. In short, everything that is stressing you out is a story mostly of your own making.

It doesn't take much to trigger the stress response during times of uncertainty (such as when you are starting a new job), and this in turn leads to self-doubt. Did I do or say the wrong thing? Maybe I should have worded it differently? He seemed annoyed.

Before you know it, this anxiety-driven thought loop continually distracts you as you replay the situation over and over again. When you're on the rumination train, it can be hard to stop mentally replaying the events and interactions that triggered you.

Shaming and blaming yourself might appear to be a beneficial way to remind yourself to do better next time, but these are difficult emotions. On one hand, it's tempting to see them as helping to keep you on track. After all, if you stop holding yourself accountable with high expectations, you'll slack off. So, it seems to make sense to keep reminding yourself of what you should have done.

Yet holding onto what we should have or could have done keeps us in a state of stress that not only feels bad, but also keeps us stuck. The next time you meet with your manager, you may be more self-conscious, and connecting from a triggered state will limit your access to your brain's "higher powers," making it less likely that you will have a successful experience.

Yes, we want to remember and learn from our mistakes, but it's also important to shift our perception from judgment to compassion.

Since it's hard to think yourself out of a rumination cycle, it's helpful to have some tools at your disposal to shift your mindset. One technique I like to use, aside from journaling, is a breathing exercise like Box Breathing (See Chapter 12 in *Breathe into Breakthrough*) or Letting Go (described on the following page). Every time your mind returns to rumination mode, and you start either replaying the past or worrying about the future, you can use this as a cue to move into a breathwork practice.

When we understand how the autonomic nervous system works, we can use regulation of the breath and movement of the body to facilitate the necessary healing to help soften the sharp edges of difficult emotions, allowing you to gradually begin to accept that these feelings can't harm you.

*"Experiencing your whole body allows emotions to spread and not be as intense. Somatic embodiment gives us more resilience to tolerate what is happening. We have less reactivity to sensory stimuli that come from both within and without."*
*—Donna Brooks, certified yoga therapist and educator*

The following practice is one I use to let go of judgment of myself, of others, or of any situation in which I'm unhappy.

**A Letting Go Breathing Practice**
*(Allow 5-10 minutes for this exercise)*

Find a quiet place where you can take a comfortable seat on the floor or in a chair. Straighten your spine, move your shoulders back and down, and begin breathing through your nose.

As your breath flows in, feel it move down into the lowest parts of your lungs, softening your belly as it moves in and out with the breath. See if you can stay tuned into the gentle pace of your breath in and out, until you feel calm and centered.

Close your eyes or soften your gaze and tune into your feelings. Identify and label your emotions as a way to downregulate them. Use straightforward descriptions like embarrassed, awkward, or angry. You can say to yourself: *You were embarrassed. You felt awkward. You were so mad your hair was on fire.* (Note my use of third-person language— this helps you separate from the intense feelings, making it easier to let them go.)

Now focus on your body and see if you can feel the place you're holding these emotions. Maybe it's the pit of your stomach, a tightening of your chest, or a flushed feeling in your face.

Keep your attention on that feeling in your body, as you continue to breathe slowly through your nose in a steady rhythm.

Now imagine breathing into your heart center as you ask yourself, where can you bring in some empathy, either for yourself, the other person, or the situation?

Now shift your awareness back to the place in your body where you were holding the tension and see if you can visualize softening that place and releasing that feeling, using your breath. Imagine yourself breathing out that stress, tension, or anxiety with each focused exhale.

Now check in with yourself, with your body. Sense the quality of presence that has emerged. You are hopefully feeling more balanced, more compassionate, and more aware of your needs.

You can think of this exercise as a rumination redirect. Every time you realize you are going down that rabbit hole, you can use this practice to adjust your perspective, and let go of the emotions that would otherwise derail you.

## Shaping Your Future

### Labeling, Intercepting, and Reframing Your Emotions

As we've seen, our limiting beliefs are based on our go-to self-defense patterns, and they're often so deeply rooted in the subconscious, we don't second guess them.

The good news is that as we continue to notice and intercept these deeply ingrained thinking habits and the obstacles they create, we have the opportunity to redirect that energy into action. Once we accept that we're capable of overcoming these fear-based obstacles and moving outside of our comfort zone, we have the power to set ourselves free to pursue our dreams.

I invite you to take a look at some common perceptions that seem so real and true, but upon closer examination, you will discover that these "truths" don't have to prevent you from pursuing your dreams.

Here are some of the most commonly used excuses as to why we can't accomplish something:

- I don't have enough time.
- I don't have enough money.
- I don't know where to start.
- I can't decide what I want to do.
- I don't know how to.
- I won't be able to.
- It never works out for me.
- I never get those opportunities.
- I'm too old.
- I don't have the right qualifications.
- I'm not (fill in the blank) enough.

This list is by no means comprehensive—there's no end to the ways our inner voice can sabotage our efforts.

Knowing you have an inner critic is one thing; knowing how to keep it from derailing your plans is another. With much of our long-held patterns happening below the radar, it's easy for deeply ingrained limiting beliefs to cause us to doubt ourselves.

Bruce Feiler, the author of seven New York Times best-sellers, including *Life is in the Transitions*, conducted a groundbreaking study on transitions. As a result, he identified three stages of change people typically report experiencing.

# The 3 Stages of Transition

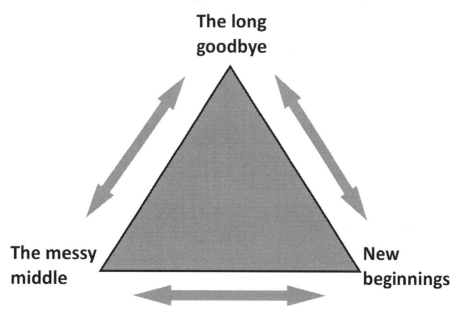

Just as life is nonlinear, transitions themselves are nonlinear. The stages don't necessarily happen in order, and everyone experiences them differently.

**The Long Goodbye**

Every transition starts with an assessment of a current way of doing or being, and then letting that way go.

This process often leads to a sense of loss, which can bring up difficult emotions, from guilt to sadness to fear, which add an additional layer of challenge. Letting go of things that have served us is never easy.

**The Messy Middle**

Letting go of old beliefs, habits, behaviors, relationships, or other ways of being can leave us feeling lost. This stage requires careful forethought and backup plans for managing the uncertainty, the inevitable setbacks, and the second-guessing of ourselves we're likely to experience. This stage usually lasts longer than we think it will, so resilience and perseverance are especially important here.

**New Beginnings**

As people explore their new ways of being they develop new understandings, personal values, relationships, and beliefs. Once this shift in identity finally takes root, the old patterns no longer hold their appeal.

As an individual moves through the stages of the transition, they begin to see a different future for themselves. With this awareness comes a sense of excitement, energy, optimism, and positivity about what's to come.

The amount of time spent in each stage varies widely as well, from no time at all to months or years. But for most of us, at least one of the stages will feel really easy, and one will be more difficult. When Feiler surveyed respondents, 47 percent said the "messy middle" was the most difficult stage to navigate. This is where most people fall off the path and abandon their goals. Among the other stages, 39 percent of people said that saying goodbye was the most challenging stage while just 14 percent named the new beginning.

When envisioning new beginnings, we're likely to feel confident and motivated. The messy middle is when our self-doubt can start to creep in. And, as we know, these self-judgments seem so true when we're on the downswing of the emotional rollercoaster ride of change.

While there is no single way to go through a life transition, we can plan in advance how we will overcome the inevitable obstacles. By examining the hidden beliefs we're likely to experience in both the initiation (goodbye) phase and the messy middle, we can learn how to work through them and stay the course.

**Shifting Beliefs Exercise**

(*Allow 20+ minutes to complete this exercise*)

The following activity is useful whenever you are contemplating a big change in your life. Give it a try right now.

What is one current goal that you really want to make happen, but where you're having trouble making progress? Example: *I want to return to the workforce after years of being a stay-at-home mom.*

_____

_____

_____

Write down all the obstacles that apply to your situation.

Examples:

- *I don't have enough time to look for a new job or find meaningful work.*
- *I can't start until I'm really certain about what I want to do.*
- *I can't count on my husband to help with the kids, so I don't have a choice.*

_____

_____

_____

_____

_____

Now, rewrite each of the limiting beliefs you identified above. This time, restructure the sentences, using the phrase "I'm resistant to," followed by a sentence or two explaining why.

Examples:

- I'm resistant to making time for my goal of finding meaningful work, because every time I look on LinkedIn, I get overwhelmed and feel like I'm too busy right now.
- I'm resistant to deciding what I want to do because I'm afraid to make the wrong choice and end up stuck in a job I hate.
- I'm resistant to leaving the kids home with my husband because I'm worried he'll resent me, or that the kids will decide he's doing a better job because he's more lenient.

Write yours here:

_____

_____

_____

_____

Can you see how all of these statements are based in fear? In reality, you do have the ability to let gradually or sometimes suddenly let go of the fear that you're avoiding by upholding limiting beliefs. It's time to replace these hidden narratives with new truths, while meeting the mean voices in your head with more understanding and compassion.

Exercise:

Choose one of the limitations you identified and answer the following questions:

Is this really true? What are some ways it might not be true? Example: *Right now, I'm responsible for getting the kids to all their activities, preparing meals, and caring for them when they are sick. My husband doesn't do much of this, but that's because he's working outside the home and I'm not. Maybe he would do more if I was working too.*

_____

_____

_____

What is the benefit of believing the faulty narrative? Safety, security, comfort? Example: *When I buy into this storyline, even though it's frustrating, I don't have to put myself out there and potentially get rejected and turned down. It's easier to keep things the way they are.*

_____

_____

_____

What does listening to this voice actually result in? Example: *I've been feeling like something is missing in my life and I'm starting to resent my husband because I'm blaming him for my situation. By keeping things as they are I'm not being challenged and I'm missing out on discovering just what I'm capable of.*

_____

_____

_____

Complete this process with all the obstacles that are preventing you from reaching your goal. You can use the pages at the end of this book to write your ideas, or any other journal you are using.

**The Passion Trap**

I can't tell you how many people I know and how many clients I've worked with who are waiting for a clear, passion-driven vision of what they should do with their lives. They end up getting stuck in the status quo because they're afraid if they choose the wrong direction, they'll miss the one chance they have to find purpose and fulfill their true potential.

And so, they wait for a sign, the perfect opportunity that this is it. The problem is, even when you've decided you found your perfect goal, your old habits will pull you back every chance they get. Remember, these old habits are such deeply ingrained neural pathways that they've become your default mode. Add to that the fear of change that puts the survival brain in high gear which triggers the inner critic to start chiming in. So, whether you're stressed, or just not paying attention, it's hard not to fall back to your old behavior patterns.

Yet here is what Stanford professors and *Designing Your Life* authors, Dave Evans and Bill Burnett have discovered. Too much focus on finding your passion could be keeping you stuck in indecision. With that much pressure, who wouldn't fold? This happens for two reasons:

**1. Most of us have more than one passion.** Waiting for passion to strike is not a very effective strategy because you might have more than one passion, which leads to analysis paralysis. You might have multiple paths you could follow, and the sheer volume of options stops you from making a choice at all. This is where most people get stuck.
**2. Passion often develops from mastery**. Sometimes we have to learn how to do something well before we can be passionate about it. It's hard to have passion about something you find challenging, even if you like to do it.

The next exercises in this workbook provide a process for assessing your goals based on your strengths and values. By considering your core values and keeping your strengths in the forefront of your mind, you're way more likely to choose a new direction, whether that's in your career or personal life, that aligns with both your inner desires (passions) and external needs.

**Designing Your Life: Setting the Right Goal**

Many people (maybe even you) have big ideas about what they'd like to achieve, but never take any steps towards their goals because they feel like they just don't have enough time. Sometimes it helps to be reminded that we all have the same number of hours per week. So, if you don't have time for your goals, how are you choosing to spend your time instead? If you're not sure, don't worry, there's an exercise for that coming right up.

To help you gain clarity, *Designing Your Life* authors have identified what they call the four main indicators of life satisfaction. The idea is if you're fulfilled in each of these key areas, you've got the recipe for a happy and meaningful life.

The four parts that make the ideal whole are health, work, play, and love. If you're lacking in some areas and overdoing it in others, your life will feel out of balance, or worse. Ever meet a workaholic with a happy home life and supportive community? The issue is we only have so much time to focus on the things we say we care about.

With this in mind, I'll share one of my favorite Life Design-inspired exercises. This activity will provide insight to help you get clear on your goal. The idea is to start where you're at, and in order to do *that,* you have to assess where you *are.*

**Let's review the categories:**

**Work** refers not only to employment, but to anything in your life that fits that definition. Cooking, cleaning, driving kids, making appointments, dealing with in-laws (not mine, of course), you name it. If it's done out of obligation, it's work.
**Health** refers to exercise, sleep, nutrition, self-care, and physical and mental health.

**Play** is what you do for fun: social outings, sports, TV, leisure activities, hobbies—things you do because you want to.

**Love** includes your relationship with yourself and others, and may include a relationship with a higher power—however you find that deep connection.

Ready to move into greater goal clarity? Begin by assessing where you are now in the four key areas, using a visual gauge-style measure that looks like this:

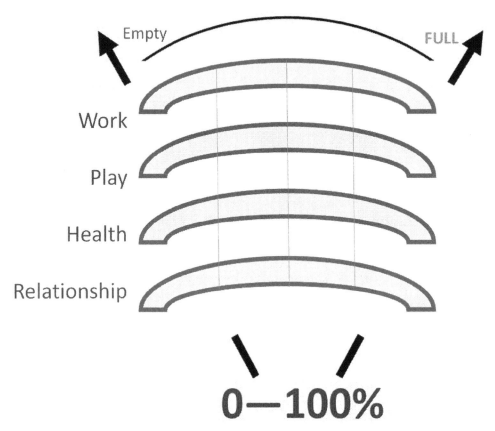

Think about your life and where you currently spend your time and energy. If you feel like a particular part of your life is exactly how you want it to be, then color in the strip to 100%. If a part of your life is only partially fulfilled—maybe you have a good relationship with your kids, but you are too busy to spend any quality time with them—then you might fill in the gauge to 40% or 60%. A perfect life would show all your areas, or gauges, at 100% for a balanced, fulfilled life.

When I start working with most people, their gauges look like this:

## Life Balance Gauge

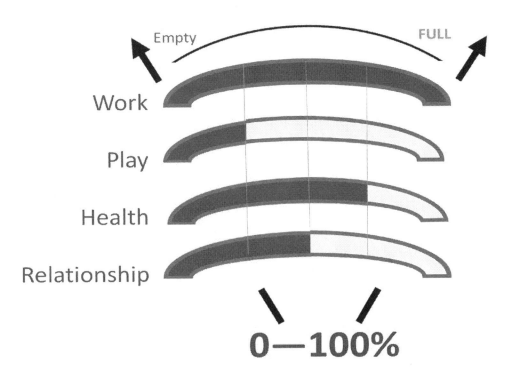

There's usually no shortage of work, but they're low in the areas of play, health, or relationship.

In my case (see above), it's pretty obvious I don't need to take on any more work, but I'm very low on play, which is detracting from my overall life satisfaction and fulfillment. So reflecting on a recent decision I made, saying yes to two days of delivering workshops to high school students was not the best use of my time, since it didn't fulfill any of my deficit areas and overloaded an area that was already full to bursting.

Prioritizing goals in the areas where you're most unfulfilled will create the biggest immediate impact. And by building up a critical component of life satisfaction, you'll gain energy and create momentum, which can then help you reach goals in your other areas as well.

While recommending more play in the context of pursuing career goals seems counterintuitive, play is one of the key life components most overlooked. In one of my favorite explorations of this topic, the authors of the 2015 NY Times bestseller, *Primed to Perform,* explore the importance of play to success at work. As it turns out, play energizes us and gives us fresh perspective, enhancing both engagement and creativity.

Setting goals doesn't need to involve adding to your workload. In fact, saying yes to coffee with friends would have been a better use of my limited time than more work ever could be.

In other words, saying yes to more work while ignoring deficits in other areas of your life isn't going to get you where you want to go. If you're always at the office but showing up drained or stressed, you're potentially undermining the hard work you're doing. Devoting attention to the parts of your life that fuel, inspire and fulfill you is as important to success as hard work. And stepping off the treadmill to re-evaluate and align all four key areas of your life is a great way to kick off your transformation process.

Time is sacred; use yours intentionally to make the greatest impact!

**Where Am I Strong?**

The Life Balance Gauge helps us recognize where we're spending our time and focusing our attention. It helps us to get some perspective on our present situation. Yet when it comes to moving forward, positive psychology suggests knowing our unique strengths and attributes helps to keep us going when we're stuck in a rut, and our nagging inner narrator keeps telling us to give up.

Using your signature strengths is associated with greater satisfaction, productivity, and engagement. Doing the things you're naturally good at leads to mastery, a proven happiness booster. Counter to popular belief, passion is often born of mastery, not the other way around.

But here's what's surprising. Most people don't recognize their signature strengths, or at least not all of them. They don't see the value in what they can do easily (sometimes because these strengths come so naturally) or all of the ways their strengths can positively impact their life.

We've taken the time to examine our values, but it's important to understand how those relate to another piece of the alignment puzzle, our character strengths. The field of Positive Psychology recognizes 24 character strengths we all share, but that show up differently in each of us. These are personality traits like love, fairness, perseverance, and creativity. While these strengths are universal, each person is unique in the combination of specific traits that come naturally and make them feel energized and engaged.

We're often so busy prioritizing the things we feel we *should* do that we forget to incorporate things we're naturally good at: those activities which make us feel competent, effective, and strong. Yet incorporating our strengths into our daily work and play gives our lives greater meaning, especially when they're skills that align with our values.

The Via Institute on Character reports that using four or more signature strengths at work results in more positive experiences and helps people to find purpose and meaning in their work, which makes sense. Mastery, or a high level of subject matter expertise in anything, has long been associated with positive emotions like self-confidence, self-acceptance, and happiness.

When you're learning new skills or stepping out of your comfort zone, there are plenty of opportunities to feel incompetent, clumsy, or uncertain. Luckily, you no longer need to avoid these situations because you now have some tools to help yourself manage these unpleasant feelings. Establishing a daily breath-based mindfulness practice raises your self-awareness overall. From this place of greater awareness, you're able to recognize these as judgments you can label and let go of. Beyond just letting go of negative emotions, it's important to recognize and embrace your strengths. You want to know where you're strong so that you can show up more powerfully in every aspect of your life.

The following exercise is designed to help you identify where you're naturally gifted, how you're using those gifts already, and how to tap into more of them, both for personal happiness and for professional growth.

Here's a list of the 24 universal character strengths identified in the book, *Character Strengths and Virtues*, written by researchers Chris Peterson and Martin Seligman.[7]

**Zest**: approaching life with excitement and energy; feeling alive and activated

**Grit**: finishing what one starts; completing something despite obstacles; a combination of persistence and resilience

**Self-control**: regulating what one feels and does; being self-disciplined

**Social intelligence**: being aware of motives and feelings of other people and oneself

**Gratitude**: being aware of and thankful for the good things that happen

**Love**: valuing close relationships with others; being close to people

**Hope**: expecting the best in the future and working to achieve it

**Humor**: liking to laugh and tease; bringing smiles to other people; seeing a light side

**Creativity**: coming up with new and productive ways to think about and do things

**Curiosity**: taking an interest in experience for its own sake; finding things fascinating

**Open-mindedness**: examining things from all sides; not jumping to conclusions

**Love of learning**: mastering new skills and topics on one's own or in school

**Wisdom**: being able to provide good advice to others

**Bravery**: not running from threat, challenge, or pain; speaking up for what's right

**Integrity**: speaking the truth and presenting oneself sincerely and genuinely

**Kindness**: doing favors and good deeds for others; helping them; taking care of them

**Citizenship**: working well as a member of a team; being loyal to the group

**Fairness**: treating all people equally; giving everyone a fair chance

**Leadership**: leading your group or team to collaborate effectively in the pursuit of common goals

---

[7] Peterson, Christopher, et al. *Character Strengths and Virtues: A Handbook and Classification.* Oxford University Press, 2004.

**Forgiveness**: forgiving those who've done wrong; accepting people's shortcomings

**Modesty**: letting one's victories speak for themselves; not seeking the spotlight

**Prudence/Discretion**: being careful about one's choices; not taking undue risks

**Appreciation of beauty**: noticing and appreciating all kinds of beauty and excellence

**Spirituality**: having beliefs about the higher purpose and meaning of the universe

**VIA Character Strengths Assessment** (*Allow 10-15 minutes to complete this exercise.*)

The VIA Survey of Character Strengths is a free survey developed by leading positive psychology researchers that assesses your top strengths, based on a list of multiple-choice questions.

Go to www.viacharacter.org to complete the character strengths assessment. Click on "Take the Free Survey."

When identifying strengths, it is important to remember that every assessment can only address a limited set of attributes. An assessment of this type provides a good starting point rather than an exhaustive list, so if you know you're strong in other areas not included in the survey, go ahead and add those character traits to the list.

Pro tip: once you have your finalized list of strengths, send it to a few people who you know well and trust to be objective, and ask if there are any additional strengths they would use to describe you. You might be surprised by the strengths others recognize in you!

List your top 3 VIA survey strengths on the lines below:

_____

_____

_____

List any other personal or professional strengths you identify with that were not part of the VIA list:

_____

_____

_____

Which of your strengths feel most relevant to you right now?

_____

_____

_____

Now take some time to think about how you're currently using your strengths.

When you reflect on your character traits, which strength makes you feel the most powerful or secure?

_____

_____

_____

_____

_____

How does this align with your values?

_____

_____

_____

_____

Now that you've taken some time to reflect on the ways you show up most powerfully, and how these strengths align with what's most important to you, it's time to weave this perspective into your life story.

## Part 3

## Telling Your Story

Writing invites us to examine the events, question the motives, and notice the patterns we have accepted as real, true, and necessary. When we get things out of our heads and onto the page, we often see a bigger picture perspective.

One client told me about her former boss, describing him as a jerk who refused to give her a referral. He ignored at least three emails before she finally gave up. I could see how her negative recollection was tainting her story.

When I asked about their working relationship, she seemed surprised to remember that he had publicly acknowledged her work on a project and always gave her positive performance evaluations. She had forgotten that part after filing him under 'jerk' in her memory bank.

When she reflected on her initial knee-jerk assumption, she realized she could have just as easily remembered him as a strong supporter of her work who probably doesn't check his spam filter. Which version would you choose?

Writing invites us to look at a more complete story than the one most readily accessible in short term memory. It also helps us to examine beliefs we haven't questioned in a while, and to decide whether they're still serving us.

The following comprehensive writing exercise is designed to help you break down your life into the most defining pieces, giving you the opportunity to look at your narrative objectively, in order to create a new narrative that will be more empowering and motivating.

**Getting to Know Your Inner Author Exercise**

*(Allow at least 45 minutes to complete this exercise)*

You will need a quiet span of uninterrupted time for this exercise. Find a comfortable space and begin with at least 5 minutes of deep breathing practice, such as Soft Belly (page 23). This helps you to transition out of whatever you were paying attention to and to come into the present moment, ready to fully focus on the exercise.

Use the following prompts to begin some reflective journaling, writing about personal feelings or experiences that you don't intend to share unless you want to. This is a way to initiate self-reflection and put feelings into words to help you better understand them.

How would I describe myself?

_____

_____

_____

What do I most want in life?

_____

_____

_____

What are some current obstacles, including emotional, that are keeping me from the thing or things I want most?

_____

_____

_____

To overcome those obstacles, what would I need to let go of or how would I have to change?

_____

_____

_____

What feelings came up as you answered the last two questions?

_____

_____

_____

## Rewriting the Future

We know habit change is hard to maintain, because so much of our behavior happens without our conscious attention. For instance, I wasn't paying attention to the way I was sitting while writing this, but in deciding to include this example, I checked in with my posture. Luckily, because I'm in the habit of practicing good posture, I wasn't slouched. Had I not intentionally intervened on a natural physical tendency and taken the time to build that habit, I would have been.

Yet that's only one challenge. The other, for many people, is deciding which one of the paths they're considering is the right one. And because they're not 100% sure which path that is, they postpone getting started until they are.

Does this sound like someone you know? Moving out of your comfort zone and into the unknown is challenging! Most of us wrestle with everything from distractibility to imposter syndrome as we try to navigate an open landscape in search of clear direction.

Your perspective, or mindset, along the path of this unmarked journey, can swing radically, from overwhelmed by too many options to trapped with zero possibilities, as you try to figure it out. Either way, it can feel impossible to make a move forward.

If this resonates with you, you may be wondering how these feelings can be so common, given how much individual circumstances vary.

The problem isn't the circumstances themselves, it's the feeling of stress that change evokes. That's the sneaky thing about stress-induced overwhelm, it feels entirely circumstance-driven, reasonable, and justified. But no matter how bad the circumstances, becoming aware of and managing your emotions is the way to clarity.

As we know, stress is a whole-body experience. So now, because you are pushing yourself out of your comfort zone on a regular basis, you're sleeping less, possibly relying on short-term escapist habits to avoid thinking about the challenges ahead, and ultimately driving your mind and body into a higher level of stress, which results in a deeper sense of stuckness.

As you can see, the feeling of overwhelm isn't due to your particular circumstances, too many or not enough options, or your inability to commit, get started or finish—it's the result of stress. Until you learn how to manage it, the survival brain will continue to have its way with you, keeping you too overwhelmed and uncertain to cope with the growing pains that come with leaving your comfort zone.

Of course, the daily practices you're learning will enable you to reduce the survival brain's dominance, but those defense mechanisms are strong, and they'll continue to pop up. Not to worry! As you continue with these exercises leading to greater self-awareness, you'll build the clarity you need to overcome these hidden defenses.

**The Three Whys Exercise**

*(Allow 10+ minutes to complete this exercise)*

This exercise helps determine what is really driving you to make the life change you're considering. Use this process to identify compelling reasons to stay committed to your goals. As you go through the following levels, you'll go progressively deeper into your strongest motivation, the one you can leverage to build clarity, focus and perseverance.

Think back to the work you did to identify what you want most in life on page 57.

LEVEL 1:

Why is it important to you?

_____

_____

_____

LEVEL 2:

Why is (Level 1 answer) important to you?

_____

_____

_____

LEVEL 3:

Why is (Level 2 answer) important to you? How does it track back to the values you identified (on page 33)?

_____

_____

_____

What might your life be like 20 years from now if you do make this change?

_____

_____

_____

What will your life be like 20 years from now if you *don't* make this change?

_____

_____

_____

Now consider why you haven't been able to make this change yet. Which emotions come up when you think about the challenges or obstacles holding you back?

_____

_____

_____

The feelings triggered by the survival brain can be powerful enough to force us into a defense response. So, we either avoid those unpleasant feelings by staying too busy (and overwhelmed) to address them, or we deflect those feelings by falling into victim mode by blaming our shortcomings, someone else, or our circumstances for keeping us stuck.

Yet as you probably know, these feelings are self-perpetuating. Avoidance and overwhelm actually increase those very same feelings. So, getting clear on what your goals are and why you want to achieve them will give you the direction and motivation and inner strength for moving into the how.

**Pro tip: Listen to your self-talk!**

One day, about a year into my daily breathing practice, I got stuck in a bout of heavy traffic. I was cutting it very close for a meeting and feeling stressed. Gripping the steering wheel, I was getting more and more agitated when an old script popped up in my head, "Why does this always happen to me?" the voice whined before I could stop it.

"Hello, victim!" interrupted my thinking brain, bringing awareness to the rabbit hole I was entering. I quickly noticed the voice, labeled the emotion, and began focusing on my breath. I moved into a Soft Belly breathing pattern, counting evenly in and out. I consciously relaxed my grip and adjusted my posture. Feeling calmer and more in control, I navigated the traffic and just made it to my meeting, which, ironically, had been postponed. Instead of beating myself up for any number of reasons, I celebrated being aware of my thought patterns and having the ability to shift from victim mentality to rational mind.

This work takes time, but it also has the ability to change your life, and eventually you will enjoy and appreciate the process along the way.

**Mindful Journaling**

*"Until you make the unconscious conscious, it will direct your life and you will call it fate."*
—Carl Jung

So much of our behavior is on autopilot. We continue moving forward from one thing to the next, without stopping to examine the feelings that are driving our behaviors. When we can bring to light the subconscious programming that shapes our perceptions, we can begin to see the hidden judgments of ourselves, of other people, and of our circumstances that make up the framework of our story.

The act of mindful journaling is writing down your story so you can examine it piece by piece. You can look at the beliefs shaping your narrative so you can decide whether or not they serve you.

Right now, when we rub up against our limiting beliefs, we're programmed to react from the survival brain. After all, those neurons have been firing together for a long time. However, when we stop and get curious about the feelings associated with the judgments, whether it's fear of failure, guilt for letting someone else down, or any number of things, we discover that our fear of the feeling is worse than the feeling itself.

In short, when we shine a light into the darkness of our mind, we can see how our old survival brain patterns escalate negative feelings to keep us safe in the comfort zone. Journaling helps us put emotions into words, which, as explored in *Breathe into Breakthrough,* is a way to reduce the anxiety associated with difficult feelings.

Once we develop a greater awareness of our difficult emotions, when they come up, we can use a practice known as labeling, which is just that, naming your emotions. When we label our emotions, we move out of the survival brain and into the region of the brain responsible for language, creating space that will prevent us from reacting to our feelings with our habitual response.

As you know, it's hard to think your way out of negative emotions. This is where you can use breathwork, or mindfulness, or one of the many other practices that move us from survival mode into the more advanced parts of the brain where we can assess our response and identify more options.

Noticing the judgments, or negative perceptions, as they come up, labeling them, and, where you can, finding compassion for these feelings before letting them go using a breathing practice, is the path from survival to thinking brain. Once you have tapped into your thinking brain, you can do a reality check and assess what's really going on.

For example: You're sitting across the table from your partner at a dinner party. You share a story with the group and notice your partner makes a weird face as you finish. All evening you're ruminating on that look, wondering what you said that was so irritating or whether your tale was simply boring.

You're feeling embarrassed and uncomfortable; your heart is racing and your palms are sweating. *Maybe it's just better for me to fade into the woodwork,* you decide. You spend the rest of the night disconnected from the group and waiting for the time to pass so you can return to the safety of your home. Another evening ruined.

As you're driving home from the party, feeling hurt by your partner and bad about yourself, she mentions, *I love that you shared your story. I know the host really related to it, after what he's going through. Sorry if I looked like I was crying for a minute there, I had something that felt like a stick in my eye. It was so painful - luckily it was just an eyelash.*

Now you're feeling better and foolish all at the same time. Good thing you didn't speak first, or the mood on the car ride home would have been very different.

How different would the night have been if you had taken a moment to breathe through your emotions, label them and just let them go? You would have recognized the assumptions you were making, at which point you could have asked your partner what was going on or just decided that, even if they didn't like your story, it wasn't a big deal and you could carry on with your night, enjoying yourself as before. Mindful breathwork gives you the power to change outcomes.

How many of us can relate to this story? In the book, *Mindwise: Why We Misunderstand What Others Think, Believe, Feel, and Want,* author and research scientist, Nicholas Epley, shares countless stories and examples of our common yet flawed beliefs.

The reality is, there is a big gap between how well we *think* we know others, and what they're feeling, thinking, and focused on at any given moment, and how well we *actually* do.

I mean, is this insight really that surprising? Probably not for anyone who has ever given a gift to a teenager. You were so sure they would love it!

So, the next time you catch yourself spinning a story based on assumptions, especially a story that makes you feel bad, stop. Breathe yourself down from that cortisol cliff, identify and label your emotions, and then let it go. Goodbye self-doubt. I don't have time for you. I'm moving on to other things. Offer some compassion to that place in you that needs it, maybe that place of insecurity about this new path. And place your trust in your strength and vision.

Whenever you question your perceptions, you're able to look at your subconscious programming, the narrative driving your beliefs. Being able to move beyond negative assumptions and consider a broader range of possibilities is the first step on the journey outside of your comfort zone!

**Reinterpreting Your Story**

In many Eastern philosophies, the goal is to view events as neither negative nor positive, but to live in the present, free of judgment. Here is one of my favorite examples of this idea, conveyed in an old Taoist story from the children's book, *Zen Shorts,* by Jon J. Muth:

> *There is a story of an old farmer who had worked his crops for many years. One day his horse ran away. Upon hearing the news, his neighbors came to visit. "Such bad luck," they said sympathetically. "Maybe," the farmer replied.*
>
> *The next morning the horse returned, bringing with it three other wild horses. "How wonderful," the neighbors exclaimed. "Maybe," replied the old man.*
>
> *The following day, his son tried to ride one of the untamed horses, was thrown, and broke his leg. The neighbors again came to offer their sympathy for his misfortune. "Maybe," answered the farmer.*

*The day after, military officials came to the village to draft young men into the army. Seeing that the son's leg was broken, they passed him by. The neighbors congratulated the farmer on how well things had turned out. "Maybe," said the farmer.*[8]

When we look at the stories we tell ourselves, how they were formed, and how they shape us, we can begin to see how they're not always so accurate. And they're always open to interpretation.

Your brain creates stories out of life experiences, often amplifying the negative and putting you at the core. It's easy to take these fear-based stories as fact and adapt our self-image and habitual responses based on this narrative. Mindful journaling gives us the opportunity to step back and objectively review the inner assumptions that may have been undermining us for years.

Now that we know ourselves, our values, and our strengths, we're able to weave them into this new narrative. From this new perspective, we have the opportunity to approach our story more intentionally. We can use what we've learned are our best assets and find the support we need to overcome the obstacles, as we rewrite our story from a place of strength.

---

[8] Muth, Jon J. *Zen Shorts*. Scholastic, 2005.

## Part 4

## Standing Up for Yourself

**Connecting with Your Power Zone**

I love the idea of a power zone, a source of inner strength and energy available to each of us. By embodying the traits and characteristics that make us strong, we can connect to that source when we need it, like anytime we're about to step out of our comfort zone.

As we've seen, the breath connects the brain with the rest of the body as these two systems work to stay in sync. It's also important to note that emotions, which we typically assign to the mind, also live in the body. We rarely think of emotions like happiness or disgust as body-based, but scientists have created a colorful map to prove it.

A team of scientists in Finland studied over 700 participants, using a unique topographical self-report method. In a series of five studies, participants were shown two silhouettes of bodies alongside a series of emotional words, stories, movies, or facial expressions. They were asked to color the bodily regions whose activity they felt increasing or decreasing with each emotional cue.

Researchers found that the results were surprisingly consistent, even across demographics and cultures. The maps below illustrate where emotions ranging from the highs of excitement to the lows of depression show up for most of us. It's interesting to see the overlap between positive and negative emotions, illustrating how our interpretation of these feelings determines how we experience them.

Here's an example: you have a feeling, like a stomach full of butterflies when you think about going to the networking event you signed up for last week. You immediately interpret this signal as dread, which reminds you of how anxious you feel about networking, so you decide not to go. The next day you immediately regret it.

I used this example because it's so common. Yet simply knowing that you have a choice in how you interpret and respond means you can pick the interpretation most aligned with your breakthrough goals. If I can decide whether the butterflies either mean dread or excitement, why not choose the option more aligned with my goals? An added bonus: as I get ready to attend the event from this place of excitement, my stress level will drop a notch too!

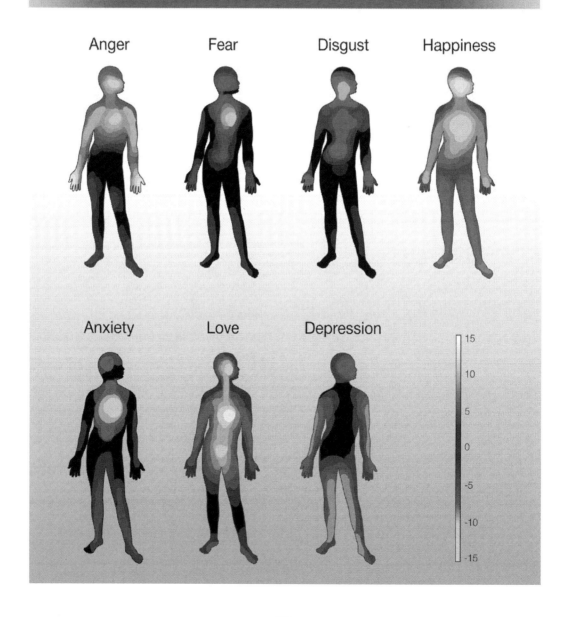

Now it's your turn! When you look back at the questions you answered on pages 57-58, about the emotions that come up when you think about the obstacles you're encountering, can you feel where those emotions show up on your body?

If so, you can use the diagrams below to shade in those places.

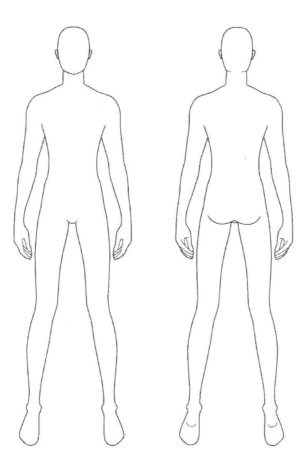

What's important to note here is that the body feeds emotional signals to the brain, which in turn sends those feelings back to the body, in an ongoing feedback loop that will continue to increase those emotions (both good and bad) until the feedback loop is interrupted in some way.

You've already seen how the breath can help you access your thinking brain to allow you to think more rationally. Now we'll explore some of the ways you can use movement to interrupt this feedback loop as well.

Social psychologist, Amy Cuddy, was among the first to research the way certain physical postures, or "power poses" affect our brains and behaviors. Holding certain postures for at least 5 minutes increases testosterone levels, raising your confidence right along with it. Pretty helpful right before a presentation, first date, or a job interview, don't you think? UCSC professor, Antonia Damasio, is another researcher who theorizes that each emotion activates a distinct region of the body, and the subconscious recognition of those patterns helps us consciously identify that emotion.

When you realize your brain is "listening," you can understand why the way we hold our bodies matters so much. Whether we're hunched over while preparing for an important presentation or slouched in a classic defensive posture to instinctively protect our internal organs from a perceived threat, our body is signaling our subconscious selves that we are not safe. Suddenly we feel anxious or stressed and assume it's because the presentation is so important, when the reality is that our body posture is exacerbating our negative feelings. We're creating a mind-body feedback loop without even realizing it.

However, if we stand tall, or sit up straight with our shoulders back, we'll feel stronger and more confident, as our body sends signals of safety and control. It is the perception of being in control (rather than the reality of being in or out of control) that's an important buffer of negative stress.

According to some studies, stress is not a simple response to an emotional trigger; rather, it's a bodily sensation that you interpret based on factors like past experience and your current state of mind, which is why people intentionally do daring, scary, or dangerous things for no other reason than the thrill of it. They've interpreted the normal fear of jumping out of a flying object thousands of feet off the ground as an adrenaline rush, rather than abject terror.

When you're aware that stress is normal and open to your interpretation, you have the chance for a different outcome.

One classic example is public speaking. Easily the top-ranked fear for most people, with practice, you can learn to change your experience of the adrenaline butterflies from fear to excitement. The feelings are the same, but when you notice the butterflies begin to flutter, before reacting in the usual way, you can take a breath and choose to interpret them differently.

As we have learned, the breath is the bridge between mind and body. When we become more aware of our physical selves, we recognize our ability to control how we interpret our bodily sensations. Is it fear or excitement? Risk or challenge? Failure or part of the learning process?

We can also use our bodies to influence our emotions and show up more powerfully. Research reveals we can change other people's perceptions of us—and even our own body chemistry—simply by changing body positions.

*"How you feel depends on the way you use your brain, not the circumstances you're in."*
—Jill Bolton Taylor

As you become tuned into the signals your physical self delivers, you'll learn not only how to reinterpret them to your advantage, but also how to access the positive emotions you need to stay on track when the going gets rough.

While it's unrealistic to believe we can change all of our pain states into positive emotions just by reinterpreting them, we don't have to succumb to our negative feelings either. Recognizing where our sources of natural strength reside is another way to use the physical channel to stay strong and resilient through emotionally painful situations.

The following exercise builds on work you did earlier in the book. Refer back to the VIA Character Strengths exercise on pages 53-54. Select the strength that you identified as your most powerful. Read on to learn how to tap into this strength to build your resilience during times of uncertainty.

**Embodying Strengths Exercise**

*(Allow yourself 20 -30 minutes for this exercise)*

This mind-body exercise helps you to embody your greatest source of strength, so you can build upon it to gain the energy and momentum to either get started or keep going on the path to your true purpose.

**You'll need:**

- A pen
- A cushion or comfortable place to sit.
- Some space for standing movement

We'll begin with a writing exercise.

Describe how the strength you identified carries you or helps other people:

_____

_____

_____

Think of a time you were successful as a result of leveraging this strength. What does this say about you?

_____

_____

_____

Think of a recent challenge that you faced and overcame. How did you use this strength to handle it?

_____

_____

_____

Put your pen down and take a minute to visualize yourself back in that specific moment in as much detail as possible. Where were you? Who were you with? How did you feel?

Now, close your eyes and mentally scan the regions of your body, starting from your feet and moving up to the crown of your head, just briefly noticing what you feel. Can you identify the place in your body that becomes energized when you connect with your source of strength?

**For example:**

_I was able to tap into my passion while I was leading a group meeting. I'm picturing how powerful it felt. My heart was beating fast and high in my chest, was sweating a bit, and I felt like my brain was on fire from all the ideas buzzing around._

Now it's your turn:

_____

_____

_____

Hang on to that powerful feeling! We'll be harnessing it in the next activity.

**Tap into Your Power Zone**

I have described this exercise below, but it is best if you can listen to the process while you are participating. Go to www.elizabethborelli.com/the-resilience-toolkit/ for a video demonstration.

Come to a standing position, with hands by your side, shoulders relaxed, feet hip-width distance apart, facing forward.

Move your awareness to the ground beneath your feet. Your stance is relaxed here, knees can be softened. Feel into all four corners of your feet as you connect with the ground beneath you.

Now begin a soft belly breathing pattern. You can place a hand on your belly, as you begin breathing in and out through your nose, keeping the breath low and slow. You can start breathing coherently, which simply means evenly matching the length of your inhales with your exhales, by keeping an even count of 4, 5, or six. Keep it slow and steady without straining.

Now start to bring in some movement.

Keeping the coherent breathing pattern, begin walking in place, bending one knee at a time, shifting the weight side to side, keeping the balls of your feet on the floor as you lift one heel at a time, keeping time with your breath counts.

You can start moving your hips and allow your shoulders to come along, as you continue walking in place while keeping your awareness on the coherent pace of the breath.

After 5-10 more breathing cycles, come back to standing still, feet firmly planted as we continue matching movement to breath.

Lift your arms out to your sides and then extend them straight up overhead on the inhale and back down on the exhale, keeping time with your counts.

Repeat this movement, keeping the coherent breath count.

Next, move into a side stretch on each side by placing one hand on your hip, while the opposite arm stretches all the way up and over head as you inhale. Keep your hips square and lean in the direction of your stretched arm as you complete the inhale and movement. With an exhale, return the arms and body to a neutral standing position before repeating this movement on the other side, keeping the coherent breath count.

Repeat once more on each side.

After returning the arms and body to a neutral standing position, raise your arms straight out to either side as you sweep all the way up, reaching for the sky on the inhale and returning back down on the exhale.

You can let go of the counting as you shift to stand with hands on hips, moving feet slightly wider than hip width distance apart. Continue to breathe through your nose, slow and low as you begin to loosen your jaw by opening your mouth wide and moving your jaw side to side.

Come to a place of steady stillness, with mouth and eyes closed, and visualize that source of strength you recognized earlier.

Return your awareness to that source of strength in your body, the zone of your body where you felt that powerful energy, where that source of power resides.

Now reconnect with your breath and visualize being able to direct your breath into that region. Imagine sending even more energy and strength into that place by using your breath. Take as much time as you need here to embody that powerful feeling.

You can even go so far as to stand up with your hands on your hips, in what Amy Cuddy calls Wonder Woman pose. How's that for the epitome of strength?

When you're finished, sit back down and take a few minutes to journal about what comes up for you now when you ask yourself the question, *where am I strong?*

_____

_____

_____

Can you identify the source of that strength by shading or circling the area in the line-drawing below?

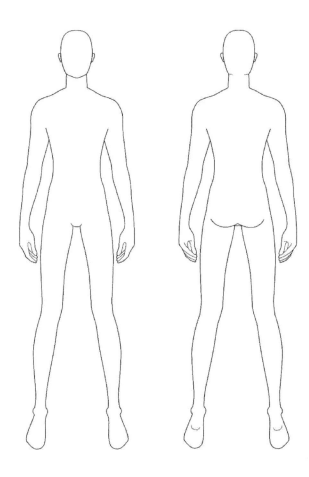

It's important to note that not everyone will make the connection between emotions and bodily sensations right away. The idea is to get accustomed to checking in with your physical state to understand where your body is helping or hurting you, so you're able to align your mind-body states in the direction of your long-term goals instead of reacting from a short-term fight-or-flight state.

If you're unable to identify the location of your feelings in your body, you can focus on connecting with your heart center, which is a source of strength you can always return to.

**Is it True? Four Questions That Can Help You Find Out**

"All the suffering that goes on inside our minds is not reality," says best-selling author and thought leader Byron Katie. Katie, as she's known, has developed a process she calls "The Work." The Work is Katie's system for freeing ourselves of the thoughts that hold us back. Based on her twenty years of high-profile experience, our greatest obstacles are just a story we entrap ourselves within.[9]

Completing 'The Work' means answering four questions that, when applied to a specific problem, enable you to see what is troubling you in an entirely different light.

The first question is, *is it true?* This question can change your life. Be still and ask yourself if a particular obstacle or perceived problem is actually true.

The second question asks you to assess the certainty of your belief. *Can you absolutely know it's true?* This is another opportunity to open your mind and go deeper into the unknown, to find the answers that live beneath what we think we know.

The next question starts to uncover the consequences of thinking in that way. *How do you react—what happens—when you believe that thought?* With this question, you begin to

---

[9] "The Official Website for The Work of Byron Katie." *The Work of Byron Katie*, 2 Feb. 2018, https://thework.com/.

notice internal cause and effect. You can see that when you believe a certain way, there is a disturbance that can range from mild discomfort to fear or panic. Notice and label the feelings that arise.

The final question prompts you to consider the benefits of thinking differently. *Who would you be without the thought?* Imagine yourself facing an obstacle or challenging situation, without believing that it is truly insurmountable. How would your life be different if you didn't have the ability to even think the stressful thought? How would you feel? Which do you prefer—life with or without the thought? Which life helps you get to a place of being more aligned with your goals and values?

After the four questions, the final step in this process asks you to *turn the thought around.* The "turnaround" gives you an opportunity to experience the opposite of what you believe. Once you have found one or more turnarounds to your original statement, you are invited to find at least three specific, genuine examples of how each turnaround is true in your life.

This process can be used to address all the obstacles in your life, both big and small. One common obstacle many people face is feeling overwhelmed, which makes it nearly impossible to commit to and follow through with our goals. We hear *want to, need to,* or *should* come out of our mouths on a regular basis. I talked about getting my Master's for so long before I actually committed, that by the time I told friends I was enrolling, they thought I had already graduated!

Why didn't I do it sooner? I told myself I wasn't sure if the program I was considering was the best or right one. Yet the program I enrolled in had been well-established for 40+ years.

I told myself I was too busy with my kids and my business to get a Master's. Yet had I just taken one class at a time back then, I would still be finished by now, without having to do it all at once! My survival brain was certainly effective at coming up with excuses, and I never reflected long enough to decide if these obstacles were really as insurmountable as I made them out to be. I wish I had known about these four questions back then. I could have used them to make a more objective assessment. The following activity will help you do just that.

## Obliterating the Obstacles

Look back at the obstacles you listed on page 57. Is there one you've been particularly stuck on? Select one that feels like something you can address. In other words, don't focus on an obstacle that is what Life Design terms a *gravity problem*. Just as we can't change gravity, we also can't change other people and we may not be able to alter our physical limitations. But with the right mindset and perspective, we can find creative ways to tackle the rest.

Write your obstacle here:
*Example: I am too busy to earn my Master's degree.*

_____

_____

_____

Use the space below to describe the ways this obstacle has been holding you back, keeping you stuck, or stopping you from committing to your goals?
*Example: I work full time, have a family to take care of, and I'm exhausted at the end of each day. I don't have the time or energy to take on more.*

_____

_____

_____

Now, ask yourself the following four questions:

**Question 1:** Is it true? How so?

*Example: Yes, it's true my days are very busy.*

_____

**Question 2:** Can you absolutely know it's true? What else could be going on?

*Example: I usually have some time on the weekends and evenings to relax, so I could use that time to study. I feel too tired to add more to my load, but if I'm learning something that I find engaging and purposeful, maybe it will fill me with more energy.*

_____

_____

_____

**Question 3:** How do you react—what happens—when you believe that thought?

*Example: When I believe I'm too busy, I feel overwhelmed and exhausted. I get tired just thinking about all I have to do, and I'm not motivated or passionate about any aspect of my life.*

_____

_____

_____

**Question 4:** Who would you be without the thought?

*Example: If I could believe I had enough time, I would feel more calm and less tired. I'd probably get more done and be more efficient with my time.*

_____

_____

_____

**Turn the thought around:** If you believe the opposite, what becomes true now? Try to find at least three.

*Example: I do have enough time to get my Master's. I can take just one class at a time, one evening a week. I can get up early on Sundays and work on homework before the rest of the family is up. Instead of going to the gym after work, I will get up an hour earlier and exercise at home in the morning. That will give me more time and energy in the evening to work on my classes.*

_____

_____

_____

_____

_____

_____

*"Whatever you do, or dream you can, begin it. Boldness has genius and power and magic in it."*
—Goethe

## Getting Out of Your Head: a Visualization Practice for Overcoming Obstacles

*(Allow 10+ minutes for this exercise)*

To begin, find a quiet place where you can take a comfortable seat on the floor or in a chair. Straighten your spine, move your shoulders back and down, and begin breathing through your nose.

As your breath flows in, feel it move down into the lowest parts of your lungs, softening your belly as it moves in and out with the breath. See if you can stay tuned into the gentle pace of your breath, in and out, until you feel calm and centered.

Think of the obstacle that you listed in the previous exercise. Maybe it's being brave enough to reach out to a former colleague as part of your networking process. Maybe it's taking the time to update your resume. Maybe it's talking to your husband about how he can best support you.

Visualize yourself in the setting, taking the action you've been avoiding, in as much detail as possible. For example: *You're getting the person's contact information, you're writing the email, you're ready to hit "send."*

    a.   Now focus on your body and see if you can feel the emotions that come up. Maybe it's a clenching in the pit of your stomach, or a tightening of your chest, or a flushed feeling in your face.

Keep your attention on that feeling, as you continue to breathe deeply. See if you can imagine softening that place and releasing that feeling, using your breath.

    b.   Now ask yourself, what could go wrong? Am I worried I may be judged negatively? Or ignored? Or told to go to hell? When I ask this in workshops it usually gets a laugh, but we don't often think through the worst-case scenario long enough to realize the worst that could possibly happen is nothing you can't overcome.

Take a moment to write down three things that could go wrong in your scenario.

_____

_____

_____

Thinking of possible negative outcomes will probably elicit an emotional response. Reconnect with your breath, consciously keeping your diaphragm engaged as you direct your awareness to the pain or tension. Deepen your breath and imagine using it to soften that holding, letting go of the tension as you release it on the out breath.

Looking back at the things that could go wrong, think of how you would handle each one of them. Really take the time to visualize each worst-case scenario and how you might handle it. For me it could be, what if my book gets a negative review? I might feel like crap, be tempted to wallow in self-pity, or second-guess myself. Or I could adopt a different perspective and calmly see what I can learn and improve upon.

Visualize yourself managing each of these challenges in as much detail as possible. You may want to take some notes here to remind yourself of your fallback plan when you need a burst of motivation.

How did it feel to overcome the potential obstacles? Can you connect with that place in your body where you feel strong? Imagine breathing energy into the source of your strength as you acknowledge your power to overcome obstacles.

## Boundaries: Letting Go of the Pleaser

One of the most common obstacles my clients face is establishing and upholding boundaries. Whether that's saying no to another assignment when you're already overloaded, or to a family member you usually say yes to, it's hard to stand your ground.

When you're working through a career or life transition, it is essential that you give yourself the time and space you need to take on these new challenges. But it can be hard to prioritize your goals when those around you have priorities of their own. And when it comes to relationships, if you're not solid and clear with your priorities, it's all too easy to get sidelined.

To be clear, the people in your circle won't all be thrilled when you shift from there-for-them to there-for-you. They may complain and even try to shame you. This is when you really need your tools. After all, you may have been putting the needs of other people above your own for longer than you now wish you had, by years or maybe even decades. If those who depend on you begin to feel neglected, just remind them of the oft-repeated advice we are given each time we take off in an airplane: you always put your own oxygen mask on first before helping others.

It will be challenging to uphold your boundaries, so you'll need to practice keeping your survival brain calm by prioritizing self-care, staying self-aware, and using breathwork to shift out of a stress response.

How can you organize your schedule to put on your mask first? One useful strategy is to first determine your most productive or creative time of day, the time when you really want to focus on your goals. Do you need two uninterrupted hours each morning to write code, project plans, or prose? Create boundaries around that time and do whatever you need to uphold your boundaries. By making a schedule that prioritizes your needs, you'll set an example for yourself and others that your time and your goals are valuable.

One role many people, especially women, fall into is that of Pleaser—the person who says yes when they really mean no, and ends up feeling used and resentful.

You can refer back to your Life-Balance Gauge (page 49) as a tool to assess where to allocate your time. When you find yourself being asked to do something that doesn't align with your goals and priorities, it's important to make a rule for yourself to make space between the question being asked and the answer. Even if it sounds fun or you feel like you have to say yes in the moment, make it a habit to take some time to think about your response before you give it. Practice taking a deep breath and saying, "Let me check my calendar," or, "I can let you know (tomorrow, next week, next year…)." Do whatever feels comfortable for you and gives you enough time to calmly assess the pros and cons of the request.

Some great questions to help you decide whether you should say yes or no:
1. Does the commitment fit with your top priority goal(s)?
2. Do you really want to do it?

If you answered no to items 1 and 2, but you still want to be helpful, consider if there is someone else you can recommend instead. It's hard to say no when people are used to hearing you say yes, so offering an alternative can make it easier.

When you want to pursue a lofty goal but you feel overwhelmed and filled with self-doubt, use a combination of breathing exercises and visualizations to calm your survival brain, quiet the negative voices in your head, and gain a clear vision of what you want to achieve. Consider the obstacles you perceive to be in your way and reframe them to make them achievable. Take whatever steps are necessary to ensure you have the time, space, and focus to prioritize your goals, even when that means saying no sometimes to friends and family. Let go of the judgment that will come up when you first do something new, and work towards your goals with confidence and strength.

# Part 5

## Your Breakthrough Toolkit

### Visualizing Success: Getting Clear on Your Goals

Every day, you have the opportunity to rewrite your story from a more empowering perspective. As you may recall from *Breathe into Breakthrough*, the practice of visualization, or mental rehearsal, is a technique used by top athletes, executives, and performers. Imagining yourself in as much detail as possible doing the work, reaching the goal, and enjoying the rewards is a proven method for helping you get there.

This is a great way to keep yourself focused on your most current big-picture goals and ensure that you'll show up and stand strong throughout the challenges that appear when reaching for your dreams.

Yet getting clarity around your big picture goals can be tricky when you're living in a reality that seems to keep bringing you down. *That's great for other people*, it's tempting to believe, *they don't have my life. I've had so many challenges. They've had more opportunities.*

When you write your life story from that place, it's hard to get clear on your options and notice all the big picture possibilities. The following exercise gives you the opportunity to examine your aspirations from a fresh perspective.

### The Power of Regret

Is your lifestyle aligned with your strengths and values? You can use the power that comes from reflecting on regret to understand what's most important to you.

Whether we admit it or not, most of us have regrets. And for most people, regrets are painful. The *one that got away,* the *should have done* or *shouldn't have said*, or that idea of *how much better life would be if only....*

But regrets have an important upside.

In the 2022 best-seller *The Power of Regret,* author Daniel Pink explores what he calls the most common emotion. Although we tend to think of regrets as negative parts of our past, we can use the information gleaned from analyzing past regrets to help us move forward. We can use the things we regret, the compromises we've made, the wrong turns, the bad choices, to, in Pink's words, "make life better."

In *The Power of Regret*, Pink references the largest sampling of American attitudes about regret ever conducted, as well as his own World Regret Survey—which has collected regrets from more than 16,000 people in 105 countries. Through this work, he identifies the four core regrets that most people have.[10]

---

[10] Pink, Daniel. "World Regret Survey." *World Regret Survey*, https://worldregretsurvey.com/.

The four categories of regret:

**Boldness**: this covers regrets about not being true to oneself or playing it too safe. This is the most common category.

**Foundational**: not putting enough time and effort into long-term stability and security needs.

**Moral**: having done or not done something you now feel ashamed of.

**Connection**: not having maintained close family and social ties or having lost touch with someone meaningful.

Research shows people tend to regret inactions more than actions, especially over the long term, while in the short term, the opposite is true.

We generally think of regrets as something negative and to be avoided, but there is an upside to regret as well. Instead of ruminating on past regrets and allowing them to weigh us down, we can choose to take what we've learned, let go of our negative feelings about our mistakes and move forward with a newfound commitment to doing better in the future.

Unfortunately, this is not usually what happens. A more typical reaction to regret is with harsh self-judgment: I can't believe I said that! I feel like such a (fill in the blank). I guess I should just stay quiet next time. Of course, all this ends up doing is making us feel bad enough to avoid the risk of putting ourselves out there, voicing an unpopular opinion, or trying something new.

By taking the time to face the discomfort of our biggest regrets, we can understand what we value the most. Just as it is in the case of emotions, there are surface regrets that tend to mask what is happening at deeper levels of our psyche. Without pushing ourselves to reflect on where our regrets are really originating, our survival brain is likely to shut down any further self-inquiry to avoid the pain of negative self-judgment.

As pioneering researcher Bessel van der Kolk, MD explains in the best-selling book, The Body Keeps the Score, trauma is a fact of life few of us escape. Veterans and their families deal with the painful aftermath of combat; one in five Americans has been molested; one in four grew up with alcoholics; one in three couples have engaged in physical violence. Such experiences inevitably leave traces on our minds, emotions, and even our biology.

And from a psychological perspective, social ostracism is as threatening to our innate need for connection as physical harm; the pain of each of these experiences uses the same neurocircuitry. How many of us avoided being left out or bullied as a child? The pain of that trauma is filed in the subconscious, summoned up any time a similar situation triggers the hidden memory. When we're able to understand the feelings behind these judgments we can begin meeting them with compassion, seeing them more objectively and working to let them go.

Of course, ruminating in regret can lead to anxiety and even depression. So, it's important to use breathwork or another mindset management practice to make sure you feel safe, emotionally and physically, in order to be able to work through this process.

For this next exercise, I suggest you take 5 minutes to practice a breathing technique, to let go of any distractions.

When you're feeling present and grounded, think back to one of your big regrets. Was it a mistake you made in a certain situation, a relationship, with your job, or with your health?

_____

_____

_____

_____

Now consider the following questions, taking notes below if it helps you to process your thoughts.

How do you imagine your life would be different had you done the above (or done it earlier in your life?)

_____

_____

_____

_____

_____

Is there a flip side to that story? As in the classic Zen tale described on page 65, can you think of an outcome that would have been negative?

For example, what if by taking the opportunity you regretted missing out on, you ended up missing your true calling (which you may still be seeking)? Or what if by asking out "the one who got away," they ended up breaking your heart, going to jail, or boring you to tears?

_____

_____

_____

_____

_____

What does your biggest regret reveal about what's truly important to you? Example: I regret not taking the job that was located in another city. At the time, I wanted to stay in a place that was familiar, but now I realize that trying new things and taking risks is something I value in my life.

_____

_____

_____

_____

_____

How can you start to close the gap between regret and possibility? Meaning, if you could apply what you learned onto a new opportunity, what would that look like? For example, I regret not having gotten my master's sooner, so I finally enrolled in a program.

_____

_____

_____

What is one action you can begin with in the immediate future?

_____

_____

_____

## Reaching Your Goals

If you're come this far, you're likely to have uncovered new insights, accessed new tools and gained clarity around how your daily habits and routines take you either closer to or further away from your true purpose.

I hope your journey into the depths of self-exploration has enabled you to understand when and why you're likely to delay getting started and will assist you in noticing when you veer off course. As you know from the *Breathe into Breakthrough* companion book, information, or even insight, doesn't necessarily lead to action.

So, I encourage you to keep the momentum going by transferring your ideas and insights into specific action items. Put these on your daily schedule to ensure your good intentions result in effective progress towards your goals.

Let's get started!

Explore your options. What new ideas, careers or ventures do I want to learn more about?

_____

_____

_____

For each option, create a list of questions you have or information you need to decide on your direction.

_____

_____

_____

Finally, make a list of people you know who can either introduce you to someone in that field or answer your questions.

_____

_____

_____

Make a list of 2-5 small steps you can take to reach your goals. These should be concrete action items that you can reasonably complete in a short amount of time. If you have a bigger goal, such as "Create a website," break it down into smaller parts: plan what information to include, select a hosting platform, watch videos to learn how to create a page, design my home page, etc....."

For example:

- Begin a morning positivity practice and make it part of your routine
- Let go of one daily activity that no longer serves you (social media, doing too much for others, perfectionistic habits)
- Make time on your calendar to begin your research and/or prioritize your goals
- Find an accountability partner and set up your first meeting or call
- Hire a coach
- Identify local organizations aligned with the goal you're pursuing
- Open a LinkedIn account and begin building a network of connections who can refer or hire you
- Research online profiles or descriptions of people currently succeeding in the space you aspire to
- Schedule at least three conversations a week with people who can help you clarify, map out and move forward in reaching your goals

Make your list below. Use the pages in the back or another journal if you need more space.

_____

_____

_____

_____

_____

_____

Tips to stay motivated as you begin this work:

- Stay committed to your daily routine
- Keep your goal top of mind (with visible reminders)
- Eliminate distractions (anything that is not related to your goal)
- Connect with individuals or communities pursuing similar goals
- Use a journal to reflect on your progress and work through any obstacles along the way
- Celebrate wins!

Now you have identified your goal and committed to taking the steps to get you there. But change is not always that easy to implement.

**Rewriting Your Story**

(*Allow 20-30 minutes for this exercise*)

> *"If your dreams don't scare you, they are too small."*
> —*Richard Branson*

The way that you routinely explain your life circumstances to yourself is called your **explanatory style**. As you well know, some people tend to be more optimistic while others view the world through a more pessimistic lens. Our explanatory style reflects our natural tendencies. For example, let's say you apply for a job but never get called in for an interview. Someone with a pessimistic explanatory style would tell the story like this: *I'm just not qualified to do any kind of job. I can't even get an interview, how will I ever get a job? Those jerks probably didn't even read what I wrote on the application. What a waste of time.* In contrast, someone who is more optimistic in their outlook might frame it like this: *I guess that job just wasn't the right one for me. Well, at least I got my resume updated and I can probably use the cover letter again, with just a few changes. Next time I'll invest more time learning about the company and maybe follow up with a call.* Same experience, but you can probably see how the second explanatory style will lead to a better future outcome.

Maybe writing a more optimistic version of your life's story seems like a way of avoiding reality. Perhaps you believe it doesn't matter how you word it, your life is what it is. Positive psychology research says otherwise.

Studies have found that an optimistic explanatory style is more significantly associated with higher quality of life than either age or gender. In fact, one study of post organ transplant patients, a group typically challenged with an extensive recovery process, suggested that quality of life can be significantly affected by personality characteristics such as optimism.[11] Conversely, a pessimistic explanatory style has been found to be significantly associated with self-reported depressive symptoms.

It's important to remember that most of us are neither absolute pessimists nor absolute optimists. For most of us, our explanatory style lies somewhere in the middle of these two extremes. And the good news is, we can build resilience by reframing our personal story from a more optimistic perspective, learning to let go of our limiting, negatively-skewed story piece by piece, just like we learned to let go of old thought patterns.

In a sense we're all authors, or at least narrators. We process information by translating events into meaning. But meaning is subjective. So, our stories are highly biased as a result.

---

[11] "PositivePsychology.Com - Helping You Help Others." *PositivePsychology.Com*, 6 May 2019, https://positivepsychology.com/.

And guess what?! If you're hungry or stressed, or didn't get enough sleep, your story will probably take on an even more negative slant.

If your natural bias toward safety makes you interpret things in terms of a threat, and especially when you're tired, hungry, and stressed, how likely are you to perceive a coworker's neutral comment as a criticism, or someone's furrowed brow as a sign of how they feel about you?

And if these small actions happen to trigger a difficult memory? Hold the phone, all bets are off. Now you might think the whole world is against you, and you'll believe and behave accordingly, increasing the likelihood that your predictions will come true. This is an extreme example of a tendency that ranges the spectrum from mildly pessimistic to full blown depression, yet it's a habit that can be addressed and turned around.

People with an optimistic explanatory style feel a greater sense of control over their circumstances, rather than feeling like a victim of fate. Thinking optimistically allows them to see opportunities where others see threats. They're less afraid of change or uncertainty and they take more calculated risks and achieve greater returns as a result.

What if you could step out of your storyline and look at your life without the natural negative bias we often gravitate towards; one that's especially present during times of change? If you were coming from a place of strength and optimism, would things look different?

Think back to the last time you had a strong negative reaction to something. It could be something small, like getting cut off on the freeway, or bigger, like a fight with your spouse or a work project that flopped.

See if you can reframe the experience using a more optimistic explanatory style. What else might have been going on with that person who cut you off? Was that fight really about something important, or was it mostly two tired and stressed people letting off steam in the company of the person they love the most? What did you learn from your failed project that will help you do better next time?

Try it here:

_____

_____

_____

_____

_____

_____

As with all new skills, this one will take time to perfect, but once you start viewing your life through a more optimistic lens, you'll find it much easier to move through life's challenges without letting them drag you down.

Combine this more optimistic mindset with the mind-body connection that you learned to tap into your source of strength, shifting your energy as you let it carry your vision powerfully forward.

## Moving Forward with Purposeful Vision

Look back through what you discovered about yourself by completing the exercises in this workbook. What did you learn about your values and strengths? What about your tendency to self-sabotage? How did your biggest regret lead you to this place of self-discovery? How do your limiting beliefs hold you back? What will you do when that happens?

Now it's your turn to create a Vision Board.

This board is a place to summarize all you have learned in your journey thus far. You will also write your vision statement, a clear and detailed account of where you hope to be in one year's time. If you recall, having a clear vision of your goal is an essential step in the process of achieving your dreams.

Imagine it's one year from now and you've not only met your goal, you've exceeded your best expectations. What does that look like for you? Describe in as much detail as possible.

_____

_____

_____

_____

_____

_____

Use the detailed vision written above to create a 2-3 sentence vision statement that you can write on the vision board, shown on the following page. Fill in the other sections, using everything you have learned as you journeyed through this workbook.

# My One-Year Vision Board

Today's Date_____

## Looking to the year ahead,...

The strength(s) I'm leaning into:

_____

_____

_____

My priority values:

_____

_____

_____

What do I have to let go of to reach my goal:

_____

_____

_____

Use your answers to create your
vision statement below.

## My One-Year Vision Statement

_____

_____

_____

_____

_____

**Saboteurs**

(what to watch out for)

_____

_____

_____

_____

_____

_____

### Small Steps Checklist

1. Daily practice
2. Prioritize sleep

_____

_____

**Supports**

(people and resources):

_____

_____

_____

_____

_____

_____

_____

_____

Once you've completed this exercise, I invite you to take some time to move for 10 minutes or so to build some physical energy around this vision. Go for a walk, do some stretching, or do whatever you like to do to get your body moving!

Now come back to the vision board, reread your statement out loud and slowly, envisioning yourself in as much detail as possible having achieved that one-year vision you outlined earlier. Breathe into that feeling so you really embody it.

**Pro tip:** go to www.elizabethborelli.com/visionboard/ to download this page, fill it out, and post it where you can see it. It's a great exercise to revisit monthly to keep up to date with your progress.

### Troubleshooting

Here's the thing about change. It requires some heavy lifting. You will be asked to do hard things. It's intimidating to put yourself out there in bold new ways. But you have to put a stake in the ground, or as my friend Lori, the owner of a successful plumbing company says, "just put some pipe in the wall."

Start. That's the first step. Don't wait until it's perfect or until you know exactly what to do. That just gives your inner critic the time and space to begin talking.

Stay with your daily practice.

Start small, and when you come up against an obstacle, breathe your way through and come back to your place of strength.

Big things will happen, but in the meantime, you'll be challenged. As you have seen, there's no end to the ways the survival brain will try to keep you stuck in your comfort zone and prevent you from making progress. Life is full of distractions, but by teaching your thinking brain some strategies to get past the survival brain's sabotage efforts, you'll prevail and reach your goals in the end.

**Name That Distraction**

We've all got 'em. That thing you urgently need to do instead of the harder, but higher priority goal. The habit you default to when work feels hard and you need a quick breather—which then magically turns into two hours of distraction from your goals.

A serious breakthrough needs ample time to implement. It also takes momentum. In career coaching we call it "job search momentum," and the only way to be successful is by staying engaged with your plan, if not fully immersed in it. Half-assing it, as in starting, getting distracted and derailed, then starting again in a few days when you have time, won't get you off the ground.

The more you're able to manage the thoughts that will attempt to pull you away with sweet talk like, *I'll just check one thing*, or *Unless I do that errand now, I won't be able to focus*. These promises are alluring, but they're saboteurs in disguise. Weed them out and beat them at their own game, as you stay focused on your top priorities, build momentum, and begin to fall in love with your new direction. You'll know you're over the hump when the momentum feels self-sustaining and you're just there to guide it along.

As with all habits, breaking through your distractions starts with awareness. Otherwise, your default mode will carry you back into the safety zone.

Take a few minutes to explore the hows and whys of those places you're likely to get distracted, and what you can do instead.

What are your go-to distractions? These are the little things you catch yourself doing when you know you should be doing something else.

_____

_____

_____


Consider the following questions:
• Are these habits (something you regularly do, like checking your phone?)
• Are these moments triggered by difficult tasks?
• Is the distraction stress-relieving?

_____

_____

_____

_____

_____

_____


**When/Then Planning**

When you catch yourself losing focus and distracting yourself with a habit but you really want to change, you need a fallback plan. This way, if you're pulled to the kitchen, laundry room or your Insta account, save these "rewards" (yes in habit change, even folding laundry can be more enticing than stepping out of your comfort zone), until you take care of a priority action item you're feeling challenged to start or to continue working on.

For example, when I'm tempted to check Facebook after a few calls into my list of 10, then I'll wait until I've done all ten before I give myself a (strictly) 5-minute Facebook break. Instead of giving in to your distraction urge, you shelve it until you've done something productive. You get something accomplished and you get to indulge in your favorite distraction for a bit. It's a win-win.

Think about your most alluring distractions? Write down your plan for using this simple motivational practice to stay on track with your goals?

_____

_____

_____

_____

_____

_____

**Support and Accountability, Your Change Maintenance Plan**

As we discussed in _Breathe into Breakthrough_, environmental factors play a big role in habit change. You need a support system you can call upon for inspiration or advice when you need it. And equally important, it's helpful to have someone who will provide regular and ongoing progress checks based on the goals you establish. This is a huge factor in staying on track and maintaining motivation, and surprisingly easy to do. This accountability partner can be a coach, a colleague, a family member, an online community, or a friend. Setting up an accountability partnership is super simple. Just follow these five easy guidelines:

1. Find someone you trust to be your accountability partner. This should be someone who you can count on to connect with you once a week for a 5–10-minute check-in call.

Identify three people to approach as potential partners (names and contact information)

_____

_____

_____

2. When you've identified the right person, and they've agreed to their role, identify a regular time over the next 6 weeks to connect with your partner about your goals.

3. Get specific with them about the actions you plan to take to meet your goals. Write these daily actions down for them so they can keep you on track. You can do the same for your partner, if they are also working towards a personal goal.

4. Set a date and time and determine the format: phone, video conference, or over coffee, whatever is useful and easily doable.

5. Be sure to follow up on the previous meeting's action items each time you meet.

# Conclusion

Congratulations! You did it! You've finished the worksheets that resonated with you and added your action items to your calendar. You can use your vision board as a roadmap for staying aligned with your goals and priorities as you move forward through the messy middle, overcoming the inevitable obstacles life throws at you.

As challenging as change and uncertainty can be, knowing yourself, understanding the way your brain works, and using the tools to manage thoughts, energy, and emotions is key. Yet, as we know, it's the daily practice of breathwork, the intentional crossing of the bridge between mind and body, that will keep you on track to aligning your values, strengths, and vision.

Showing up for yourself every day and checking in with your body and mind keeps your intentions alive and will empower you to reach even your most ambitious goals.

Join me at www.ElizabethBorelli.com to engage with more content, access more tools, and keep moving forward on the path to breakthrough success, one deep breath at a time.

Notes:

Made in the USA
Middletown, DE
17 March 2022

62582036R00062